Contents

The sport of kings and a national passion

Horseracing has such a long history that it is difficult to pinpoint when or where it began. The Egyptians, Ancient Greeks and Romans all raced, although they usually preferred chariot to bare-back racing. They raced without saddles or stirrups, which were a later invention.

The Romans spread racing throughout their empire. Evidence shows that they raced at York, and racing motifs have been found on cups excavated at Colchester. We even know the names and number of wins of some of the Roman champions. However, British racing may have started as early as the bronze age, since a bit dating to 2000 BC suggests that horses had long been domesticated and hence quite possibly raced.

One way of telling racing's story in this country is through its long and almost unbroken association with royalty. This originated from the need to improve the native horses for use in war. Monarchs, probably from the crusader King Richard I onwards, imported the superior breeding stock which he would have seen in the East, and racing was a natural by-product of this. During the 12th century there is evidence of regular racehorse sales and races at Smithfield Market, and of races between knights on good horses for good prizes.

Massive losses of horses during the Wars of the Roses prompted Henry VIII to establish royal studs at Hampton Court (Surrey), Eltham (Kent), Tutbury (Staffordshire) and Malmesbury (Wiltshire), and he was fulsome in his gratitude to Charles X of Spain and others who sent diplomatic gifts of barbs and brood mares. Some were kept in a separate racing stable at Greenwich, and seem to have been raced informally.

Racing was not only for kings and courtiers. The 15th century saw the growth of racing elsewhere, often connected with local city corporations or the great families. The first records of meetings at Chester and York are for 1511 and 1530 respectively, but in both cases racing is probably much older. The prizes for these races were frequently silver bells, worn with ribbons by the winning horse. Elizabeth I is known to have raced at Croydon in 1574 and Salisbury in 1585 and in the same century racing took place at Carlisle, Richmond, Boroughbridge, Doncaster, Berwick, Lanark, Leith, Stirling and elsewhere. Kiplingcotes and other courses were established for local gentry and farmers, and others such as Hambleton in Yorkshire for local breeders.

Replica of the Silver Lanark Bell. The Lanark Silver Bell race was founded by King William the Lion of Scotland (ruled 1165-1214). No original bells exist, but this, a replica of a surviving bell from the early 17th century, was won in 1926. The course closed in 1977.
Gift: Mrs D.W.A. Swannell

Newmarket's association with racing began with James I's arrival from Scotland in 1603. The open heathland and springy turf suited his equestrian interests, and he was a regular visitor after 1605. Although these interests centred on hunting and hawking, he is known to have owned racehorses, to have employed two Surveyors of the Races, and to have attended a race here in 1619. Although enthusiastic he was a poor horseman with little sense of balance; sadly he also had a tendency to dribble and was never popular with his new English subjects. When the Griffin pub proved inadequate he built himself a palace and established his court here for weeks at a time.

James' successor, Charles I, inherited his father's hunting and racing interests and in contrast was an excellent horseman. He too was a frequent visitor to Newmarket. Meanwhile, numerous other courses sprang up around the country, many with their own rules and with prizes raised by subscription or the gift of a local magnate.

Racing was damped down but not eradicated by the Commonwealth. Indeed, the dispersal of the royal studs made their blood more generally available, especially in Yorkshire, where the parliamentarian general Lord Fairfax had a famous stud. At the time of the Restoration in 1660, therefore, racing was ready to take the opportunity.

Charles II was not merely an observer. He rode in races himself, set out rules, and adjudicated in disputes. Although he had interested himself in the affairs of Newmarket earlier in his reign, his twice yearly visits to Newmarket began in 1666 and took place regularly, establishing a pattern which continues today. Indeed, the Rowley Mile course at Newmarket is named after his hack. He rebuilt the Palace and established his court there, as well as his mistresses, most famously Nell Gwyn. A superb and extrovert rider, Charles showed off by racing against his courtiers and in 1666 established the Town Plate, a race with its own set of rules. He personally rode to victory in the Town Plate of 1671, the prize being a flagon worth £32.

James II had little time to devote to racing, but William III was enthusiastic and more racecourses were established across Britain. He reformed the Royal Stud at Hampton Court, made further improvements to the Palace at Newmarket and appointed William Tregonwell Frampton (1641-1727) as his 'Keeper of the Running Horses', the equivalent of his racing manager.

Frampton was to retain this post under Queen Anne, George I and George II and was therefore to hold a great deal of influence over racing at Newmarket.

Frampton arranged matches, some with the King's horses, and some with his own. He also arbitrated in racing disputes, despite his own reputation for sharp practice. For one secret pre-match trial, he arranged for his horse to carry an extra 7lb, not realising that his opponent knew him well enough also to put up 7lb overweight. The result of the actual match was a repeat of the form in the trial, and several people lost fortunes, but there was joy in Yorkshire where the winner *Merlin* was trained. Another story, thankfully probably untrue, is that Frampton's horse *Dragon* beat a mare in a match for 1000 guineas, after which the mare's owner declared that he would race her against any other mare or gelding for 2000 guineas the following day. Legend has it that Frampton immediately had poor *Dragon* castrated in order to qualify. *Dragon* beat the mare again, only to bleed to death at the finishing post.

William Tregonwell Frampton (1641-1727)
after John Wootton.
Frampton, 'The Father of the Turf',
had great influence over the sport for upwards of
thirty years. This portrait shows him surrounded by
his passions; a fighting cock, a greyhound
and a favourite horse, Dragon.
Gift: A.J. Macdonald-Buchanan Esq

During Queen Anne's reign racing settled at a new course at York and was introduced at Ascot by the Queen , but it was the Georgian era which was, in many ways, the golden period in the development of horseracing. However, the first three Georges had little interest themselves beyond creating further Royal Plates across the country, to add to those of William and Anne. Instead, it was George II's second son, the Duke of Cumberland, who became the first royal member of the Jockey Club and a constant visitor to Ascot and Newmarket. Indeed, the Duke bred both *Eclipse* and *Herod*, who were to prove so important in the development of the thoroughbred. Sadly he died the year after *Eclipse* was foaled, with *Herod* still in training.

George IV entered into racing wholeheartedly whilst still Prince of Wales, and became the first royal owner to win the Derby, with *Sir Thomas* in 1788. His visits to Newmarket came to an abrupt end in 1791. *Escape* came last in a race and the very next day won against a relatively strong field which included one horse which was placed in both races. Such was the outcry that the Stewards of the Jockey Club investigated and warned the

Ascot Gold Vase (1860)
The Gold Vase, manufactured by Garrard &
Company, was presented by Queen Victoria in
1860 when Captain Christie's Horror, ridden
by George Fordham, won the race
Anonymous loan

jockey, Sam Chifney, off the Turf. The Prince stood by his jockey, sold his stud and gave up racing as far as Newmarket was concerned. Chifney published a detailed defence but was never forgiven and died a debtor. Nevertheless the Prince continued to race elsewhere when his finances permitted. His brother, the Duke of York, won two more royal Derbys with *Prince Leopold* and *Moses*.

A third brother became William IV and showed a dutiful interest in the Turf, especially when he inherited racehorses from the Duke of York. Despite muted enthusiasm, he worked hard to improve the Royal Stud at Hampton Court and suggested many improvements for Ascot. His heir, Queen Victoria, had little interest in racing and a positive dislike of gambling. She and Prince Albert attended the Derby in the year of their wedding. They were not warmly received and the caterers ran out of bread rolls - she never returned. During Prince Albert's lifetime she attended Royal Ascot as a social occasion, but after his death never visited a racecourse again. Nevertheless the Royal Stud was re-established at Hampton Court, and after 1874 enjoyed considerable success before being completely dispersed in 1894.

Her son - the future Edward VII - adored both National Hunt and Flat racing and the social set that surrounded them. A lack of funds and parental disapproval meant he did not have his first runner as Prince of Wales until 1877, when nearing 40. He established two stud farms on his Sandringham estate in 1886 but successes were rare until the Prince bought *Perdita II*, 'the Goldmine' who bred *Florizel II, Persimmon* and *Diamond Jubilee. Persimmon*, by *St. Simon*, showed early promise and easily

won his first race, the Coventry Stakes at Ascot. However he was slow to come to hand as a three-year-old, showed mixed form in trial gallops and flatly refused to board the train for Epsom. Two horse specials went without him and he had to be literally carried onto the last one. Once in his box he walked over to his feed as if nothing was wrong. At Epsom he proceeded to win the 1896 Derby at 5-1, beating the odds-on favourite, *St. Frusquin*. This was an immensely popular win, celebrated with a shower of top hats thrown into the air.

Persimmon went on to win the St. Leger, and, as a four-year-old, the Gold Cup at Ascot and the Eclipse Stakes. He was equally successful at stud, producing the filly *Sceptre* (winner of every classic race except the Derby) and was champion sire four times.

1900 was another great year for the Prince. He won the Triple Crown with *Diamond Jubilee* (*Persimmon's* full brother) and the Grand National with *Ambush II*. After this the Prince's fortunes declined, and he might well have reduced his racing interests had it not been for his friend Lillie Langtry. Instead, he went on to win the Derby a third time with *Minoru* in 1909, shortly before his death.

George V maintained his father's racing and breeding

Head of Persimmon
(foaled 1893)
Persimmon's head, mounted by Rowland Ward of Piccadilly,
is a fine example of Edwardian taxidermy.
Persimmon earned a considerable amount of money for his
owner/breeder the Prince of Wales, and is commemorated
by a statue at Sandringham.
Loan: Her Majesty the Queen

THE RACE AT TATTENHAM CORNER SHOWING THE FALL OF THE KING'S HORSE, "ANMER."
THE PICTURE SHOWS THE HORSE, THE JOCKEY (H. JONES) AND THE WOMAN LYING ON THE GROUND

NIMBUS. CRAGANOUR. SUN YAT. SHOGUN.
GREAT SPORT. ABOYEUR. LOUVOIS. DAY COMET

THE FINISH.

THE DERBY, 1913,
WON BY
MR. A. P. CUNLIFFE'S "ABOYEUR."
AFTER THE DISQUALIFICATION OF
MR. C. BOWER ISMAY'S "CRAGANOUR."

MR. C. BOWER ISMAY'S	"CRAGANOUR" (DISQUALIFIED)	
1. MR. A. P. CUNLIFFE'S	"ABOYEUR"	
2. MR. W. RAPHAEL'S	"LOUVOIS"	
3. MR. W. HALL WALKER'S	"GREAT SPORT"	

The Derby, 1913
The suffragette Emily Davison can be seen falling under George V's horse, Anmer, in the top photograph.
Craganour came first, but was disqualified on the grounds that he had jostled the second horse, Aboyeur, to
whom the race was awarded. **Gift: Mr R. Waugh**

A CROWN DERBY.

Calendar for 1911-
Edward VII leading in his
1909 Derby winner Minoru.
Minoru was trained by Richard
Marsh. Ridden by Herbert
Jones, he won the 2000
Guineas and then the Derby by
a very short head. After the
King's death Minoru was
exported to Russia. He
disappeared during the Russian
Revolution.
Loan: R.H. Till Esq.

establishments, but had only one classic success (with *Scuttle* in 1928). It was under one of his horses, *Anmer*, that the suffragette Emily Davison died during the 1913 Derby. The Queen telegraphed her commiseration to Herbert Jones, the jockey, referring to the 'sad accident caused through the abominable conduct of a brutal lunatic woman'. Neither horse nor jockey suffered any lasting injuries.

George VI was elected to the Jockey Club in 1921 but took little part in racing until his accession in 1936. In 1942 he became leading owner, having won the wartime versions of the 1000 Guineas, the Oaks and the St. Leger with *Sun Chariot*, and the 2000 Guineas with *Big Game*. Both horses were leased from the National Stud (at that time in Ireland), trained by Fred Darling and ridden by Gordon Richards, the stable's first jockey. The King's *Hypericum* won the 1000 Guineas in 1946, trained by Cecil Boyd-Rochfort.

After the Royal filly *Avila* won the Coronation Stakes at Ascot in 1949, Lord Mildmay managed to persuade Queen Elizabeth (now HM The Queen Mother) to become a National Hunt owner. With his help and in partnership with her daughter the Queen purchased *Monaveen* to be trained alongside Mildmay's horses at the Kent stable of Peter Cazalet. *Monaveen* won nine races in Princess Elizabeth's colours, and came fifth in the 1950 Grand National. Sadly Lord Mildmay was drowned in May of that year.

HM The Queen Mother had two runners in the 1956 Grand National, *M'As Tu Vu* and *Devon Loch*, the latter ridden by former champion jockey Dick Francis. *M'As Tu Vu* fell at the 19th fence but the roar of the crowd grew as *Devon Loch* led at the last fence. Just fifty yards before the finish *Devon Loch* inexplicably spread-eagled, to be overtaken by *ESB*. As a result he is probably the most famous loser of the Grand National, but he survived to win two races the following season. Dick Francis, of course, went on to become a highly successful novelist. Wins by HM The Queen Mother are always popular, and her 400th came when *Nearco Bay* won at Uttoxeter in 1994.

Our present Queen is well-known for a serious and enthusiastic love of the Turf. To date she has had five classic successes: *Carrozza* (Oaks 1957), *Pall Mall* (2000 Guineas 1958), *Highclere* (1000 Guineas 1974) and *Dunfermline* (Oaks and St Leger 1977).

Sir Gordon Richards on Sun Chariot by Sir Alfred Munnings (1878-1959)
Sun Chariot (foaled 1939) showed so little initial promise that she was nearly sent back to Ireland, and she could be very badly behaved.
Nevertheless she won eight races including the 1000 Guineas, Oaks and St Leger, and bred 7 winners at stud. She died in 1963.
Bequest: The Executors of E. Cooper-Bland

Her best horse, *Aureole*, was second to *Pinza* in the Derby in Coronation week, won the King George VI and Queen Elizabeth Stakes, and was twice champion sire.

Both Prince Charles and the Princess Royal have ridden in races; indeed the Princess won the Diamond Stakes on *Ten No Trumps* at Ascot in 1987 and the Queen Mother's Cup at York on *Insular* in 1988. These are the two principal races for lady riders run each year. It therefore seems certain that racing will continue to be *'The Sport of Kings'*.

Her Majesty the Queen's Racing Colours (left) and the racing colours of Her Majesty Queen Elizabeth the Queen Mother (right)
Gifts: Her Majesty the Queen and Her Majesty Queen Elizabeth the Queen Mother respectively

Below: Winners Enclosure Ascot Diamond Day 1987 after HRH The Princess Royal had won The Dresden Diamond Stakes (Ladies Race) on the Michael Stoute trained 'Ten No Trumps' (Bernard Parkin, Cheltenham)

Right: The 1981 Kim Muir Memorial Challenge Cup, Cheltenham National Hunt Festival. HRH The Prince of Wales and Good Prospect take an early fence. The leading horse is Indecision, trained in Ireland and ridden by Mr C. Magnier. (Bernard Parkin, Cheltenham)

Meeting at Clifton and Rawcliffe Ings, York, Sept. 1709 by James Ross
Purchased using funds donated by the friends of the late Major David Swannell and a grant from the MGC/V&A Purchase Grant Fund

THE TRANSFORMATION OF RACING

At the start of the 18th century, most racing took the form of matches, with records kept in private match books, diaries and local records. The painting of the second race at the inaugural meeting on the new course at York in 1709 gives a good indication of the nature of the sport at the time. Five horses were entered, the winner being the first to win two heats. Each heat was run over four miles, and during the rest between heats the horses would probably have been rubbed down and revived with whisky. Only three made it to the last of the four heats which it took for the horse on the left, *Whitenose*, to become the winner. Her owner, Leonard Childers, won a trophy worth £40, which can be seen on top of the post in the left foreground. Jockeys were weighed before and after the race on scales slung from this post. Incidentally, York was the first meeting in the country which thereafter appeared in an unbroken sequence of published results.

At this period the horses would have carried heavy weights and have been at least four years old and usually more. Some horses were ridden by their owners or their friends and some by professional jockeys. Alongside the major racecourses where Royal Plates were run, there was a sea of dishonesty and small races run for tiny prizes. Betting was prodigious and blamed for the downfall of many an impressionable young person.

Matches continued to be popular throughout the 18th century. One of the most famous took place over the Beacon Course, Newmarket, in 1799. Huge crowds

Beacon Starting Post
The Beacon Course covered a distance of 4 miles, 1 furlong and 177 yards when eventually abandoned. It finished at the Duke of Portland's stand, which features in many old prints of racing at Newmarket. The course became obsolete in the late 19th century, and after 1904 was only used for the rare challenges for the Whip or the Cup over its final two miles.
Gift: Newmarket Racecourses Trust

9

A Match for 3000 Guineas between Hambletonian and Diamond at Newmarket in 1799
Print after J.N. Sartorius
(1759-1828)

Hambletonian, ridden by Francis Buckle, is shown beating Diamond, ridden by Dennis Fitzpatrick. The modern equivalent of tens of millions of pounds rested on the outcome, and all the pubs and inns for miles around were full the night before the race. The moveable judge's stand can be seen at the winning post. It was not until 1839 that others were banned from riding behind the race.
Loan: Mr D. Oldrey

gathered to see the best horse of the North of England, *Hambletonian*, meet *Diamond*, champion of southerners. *Hambletonian* was owned by the handsome Sir Harry Tempest Vane and in all won 18 races, including the St. Leger. The only time he was beaten he ran off the track at York in a race he would otherwise certainly have won. Joseph Cookson's *Diamond* had won over the Beacon Course at the Spring Meeting of the previous year, as well as numerous other races over four miles but was allowed 3lbs by his famous rival. Each owner had put up a stake of 3000 guineas and also had a bye-bet of 800 guineas. Both the betting and the race were very close, the victor being *Hambletonian*. He was ridden by Francis Buckle who, as ever, remained calm despite the huge sums that rested on the outcome.

However, in general, racing had been transformed by the end of the century. There was an emphasis on shorter distances and speed and therefore younger horses. Selective breeding adapted the type of horse to suit these new challenges.

The field in each race tended to increase for two reasons. Firstly, handicap races were introduced. An independent assessment was made of the weights to be carried by each horse according to its previous performances rather than just according to its age or height or by agreement between owners. This encouraged more owners to enter their horses, since it evened out the chances of winning; otherwise nobody would risk matching their horse against one with an exceptional record. Even so, the first notable public handicap for more than two horses did not take place until 1790 with the first running of the Oatlands Stakes at Ascot, won by Charles James Fox's *Seagull*.

Secondly, the number of sweepstakes grew rapidly from about 1770. Since each owner in the race contributed to the prize money, the total amount became worth competing for compared to the amount put in. The increased fields and shorter distances were vastly more exciting for spectators and provided excellent betting opportunities. No longer did a day at the races consist of a war of attrition between the same horses running 4, 5 or even 6 heats of a single race.

Draw numbers used by the clerk of scales
Gift: Mr Cedric Manning

This transformation of racing was almost entirely due to the influence of the Jockey Club. The Club began as a London Gentlemen's Club like any other, the term 'Jockey' at that time meaning 'one who has to do with horses'. The Club is first mentioned in 1752, the same year a lease was taken on the site of the present Jockey Club in Newmarket for the building of a Coffee Room. It soon grew into a recognised body with influence well beyond Newmarket. However, it took the Club over a century to

Detail from one of a series of paintings,
The Life of a Thoroughbred
by John Alfred Wheeler (1821-1877), showing the starter
attempting to line up the horses before dropping his flag
for the 'off'.
Purchase

centralise the regulatory and administrative aspects of racing.

The Club was run by first one and then three elected Stewards, three of whom wielded such influence that they are known as the 'Dictators of the Turf'.

Sir Charles Bunbury (1740-1821) was Steward by the time he was 28 and remained in office for over 50 years. He favoured shorter races for younger horses, and during his time the five classic races for three-year-olds were founded. He won the first Derby himself with *Diomed* and had four other classic wins. It was he who demonstrated the power of the Jockey Club by 'warning off' the Prince's jockey over the *Escape* affair, although the Club's writ did not then run beyond the Heath and Chifney rode for the Prince elsewhere.

Lord George Bentinck (1802-1848) concentrated on improving the sport for spectators and eradicating fraud and mismanagement. Horses were to be saddled in a specific place and paraded before the crowd before the start; the horses were to be numbered and greater care to be taken over weighing out and in. Judges were no longer given gifts by the winning owner. Spectators could choose between differently priced enclosures.

Bentinck also fined the clerk of the course if the race started late, and introduced the starting flag. Until then, it had been commonplace for jockeys to deliberately unsettle the favourite by causing false starts when the starter shouted 'Go!'. Flag starts only proved a partial answer but were still a great improvement.

Bentinck was indefatigable in his search for the truth regarding possible frauds and dishonesty, but as an enthusiastic owner and bettor sometimes defined his own rules. His most famous ruse was the invention of the horsebox, so that his St. Leger entry was to be seen at Goodwood days after he should have been walking to Doncaster. *Elis* arrived fresh in his van and duly won. Of course his owner had placed bets at very favourable odds.

The third Dictator of the Turf was Admiral Rous (1791 – 1877), bursting with integrity and determination. He was elected a Steward in 1838, by which time his naval days were behind him. He was in demand as a private handicapper, and became public handicapper in 1855. From 1858 until his death in 1877 he was re-elected as a Steward without a break. From the Bushes at Newmarket or from the top of the stand at other courses he would watch the races through a telescope and roar at non-triers. He also emphasised the racing of young horses and the need for

Wheel from Elis's horsebox
This wheel, occasionally on loan to the Museum, comes from
the first-ever horsebox, used to take Lord George Bentinck's
horse Elis to the St. Leger in record time in 1836.
Courtesy of Jockey Club Estates Ltd

open international competition, whilst his handling of Newmarket's finances resulted in tremendous progress after a lean period. Unlike his two predecessors his few horses were of no great ability and his dominance was based solely on his personal qualities.

The Jockey Club continued to pass rules designed to protect the integrity of racing on a number of fronts. From 1879 jockeys had to be licensed and were no longer allowed to own or part-own horses. A starting machine was first used in 1896. The then fairly recent practice of doping (to win rather than to lose) was the subject of a rule in 1903 although it was not until the 1960s that routine dope tests were introduced. After the

Second World War, camera patrol and photo-finishes brought more precision to decisions, and in 1965 starting stalls were introduced.

Admiral Henry John Rous (1791-1877)
by Sir George Hayter (1792-1871)
Admiral Rous, the younger son of the
1st Earl of Stradbroke, was the most famous of turf
administrators and reformers. The principles of his weight-for-
age handicap scale, drawn
up in 1850, are still in use today.
Loan: Jockey Club Estates Ltd.

The 1960s saw a thorough reassessment of the administrative role and structure of the Jockey Club within the wider picture of the finances and health of what had now become a large industry. The Horserace Betting Levy Board was established in 1961 to collect a contribution from off-course betting turnover for the benefit of racing. In 1968 the National Hunt Committee (which had administered steeplechasing and hurdling since 1866) was amalgamated with the Jockey Club.

Other modern-day pressures resulted in the Club licensing women trainers in 1966, and from 1973 women could be licensed as jockeys. The first women Members of the Jockey Club were elected in 1977.

Today the Jockey Club continues to set and maintain standards for racing. It employs clerks of the scales, judges, starters and veterinary officers and ensures that racecourse facilities are of a proper standard for horses and humans. The Club also grants and controls renewals of jockeys' and trainers' licences and continues to administer and enforce the rules regulating the races themselves.

Silver Candelabrum, 1866
This candelabrum with the recipient
himself at the top of the central column
formed the centrepiece of a table
decoration presented to Admiral Rous
'by the noblemen and gentlemen of the
English and foreign turf to mark
25 years of valuable zealous and
disinterested services' in June
1866. The nine-course dinner was
described as 'a simple affair'.
Loan: Jockey Club Estates Ltd.

The overall leadership and strategy of the racing industry is now in the hands of the British Horseracing Board, founded in 1993. It works to improve the financial position of racing as a spectator sport. It is responsible for race planning and the fixture list, and the collection and control of funds needed to administer racing. Its membership is drawn from representatives of the racecourses, owners, breeders and others involved as well as the Jockey Club.

Weatherbys, a family firm dating back to 1770, is responsible for the day-to-day running of racing, under contract to the British Horseracing Board. Weatherbys compiles information for each race from the initial entry through to the draw, blinkers and weights, ensuring that the list of the next day's runners is out in time. The details are published in the form of racecards and sent out by computer to newspapers and racing authorities world-wide.

Warren Hill, Newmarket 1995 (Trevor Jones)

Weatherbys has published the Stud Book since 1791, and registers horses' names, owners' colours and details, issues horse passports, and allocates weights to horses according to the conditions of each race. Its bank collects and distributes prize money for every race in Britain. Racing is now a very big industry. Racing and betting directly and indirectly employ some 100,000 people, and it is said to be the sixth largest industry in the country. It continues to place great importance on the efficient administration and integrity of all its activities, relying wherever possible on self-regulation rather than imposition by Government.

BRITISH RACECOURSES

- ⚪ FLAT
- ⚫ NATIONAL HUNT
- ◑ FLAT & NATIONAL HUNT
- ◔ ALL WEATHER FLAT & NATIONAL HUNT

Perth

Hamilton Park

Musselburgh

Ayr

Kelso

Newcastle

Carlisle　Hexham

Sedgefield

Cartmel　Catterick　Redcar
　　　　Bridge

Thirsk

Ripon　　　　Beverley

Wetherby　York

Pontefract

Haydock Park

Aintree　Doncaster

Chester　　　　　Market
　　　　　　　　Rasen

Uttoxeter　Southwell

Bangor-on-Dee

Wolverhampton

Nottingham　Fakenham

Leicester

Ludlow　　　Huntingdon　Yarmouth

Worcester　Warwick　　　Newmarket

Hereford　Stratford-　Towcester
　　　　on-avon

Chepstow　Cheltenham

Newbury　Windsor
　　　　　　Kempton Park

Bath　　Ascot　Epsom Downs

Wincanton　Sandown Park
　　　　　Salisbury　Lingfield Park　Folkestone

Goodwood　Plumpton

Exeter　Taunton　Fontwell Park　Brighton

Newton
Abbot

Map reproduced by kind permission of Kiln Kilijaro Ltd.

RACING IN BRITAIN TODAY

There are fifty-nine racecourses in Britain, staging Flat racing, Jumping (National Hunt), or both. Their historical associations and variety make them an asset to racing without equal. Most racecourses are independent, the largest group being the twelve run by Racecourse Holdings Trust, a subsidiary of the Jockey Club.

After the Guineas and various classic trials in the spring, flat racing reaches its peak in the early summer with the Oaks and Derby at Epsom, followed by Royal Ascot. July and August see numerous meetings to cater for the holiday crowds with highlights at Goodwood and York. In the Autumn the number of meetings falls but there are plenty of opportunities for the better horses at Newmarket, Doncaster and elsewhere.

Jumping takes place over steeplechase fences or hurdles, starts quietly during the summer and then reaches its climax with the Cheltenham National Hunt Festival in March and the Grand National Meeting at Aintree a few weeks later. There is also a programme of National Hunt flat races to help introduce potential stars (and a lot of slow horses!) to the racecourse.

There are other types of racing in Britain. Point to Point evolved from hunting and is still linked to it. It remains an amateur sport. Arab Racing also has passionate devotees, with meetings organised by the Arab Horse Society at various courses from May to October.

The British Horseracing Board is responsible for developing an annual Fixture List and race programme which aim to balance the needs of racehorse owners, racegoers, punters, racecourses and the betting industry. A selection of flat races each year are graded into the Pattern and segregated into Groups 1, 2 and 3 to form a series of tests for the best horses, combining appropriate distances and intervals between races for different ages and both sexes of horse. A comparable scheme operates for jumping. The European Pattern system is intended to balance racing in England, Ireland, France, Germany and Italy, and to avoid unnecessary clashes. The system started here in the 1970s and nowadays is controlled by the European Pattern Committee, to which the national Committees are effectively subordinate. The idea has been taken up by all the major racing countries round the world.

Group 1 races include all five Classics and 21 other internationally important races. The Classics are restricted to three-year-olds. They were founded separately in the late 18th and early 19th centuries and were not conceived as an organised sequence. To achieve immortality as a successful owner, breeder, trainer or jockey on the flat, it is more or less essential to have been involved with several horses which have won a Classic race. However the supremacy of the Classics is today challenged by such races as the King George VI & Queen Elizabeth Stakes, Coral Eclipse Stakes and Dubai Champion Stakes, all open to older horses. At the extremes of distance, races like the July Cup and Nunthorpe Stakes test the sprinters, and the Ascot Gold Cup is the world's supreme test of the racehorse beyond 2 miles.

Miesque winning the 1000 Guineas at Newmarket 1987
(John Crofts Photography)

The Derby

First Race: 1780
Usual Location: Epsom Downs, Surrey
Current Distance: 1 mile 4 furlongs
Age: 3 year olds of both sexes but excluding Geldings
Weight: Colts 9 stone, Fillies 8st 9lb

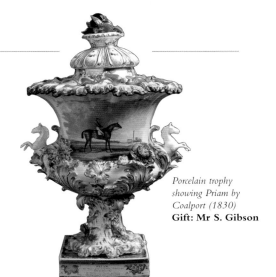

Porcelain trophy showing Priam by Coalport (1830)
Gift: Mr S. Gibson

The Derby was traditionally so-called after the 12th Earl of Derby won the toss of a coin with Sir Charles Bunbury for the honour of naming their new race. The first race, however, was won by Bunbury, with *Diomed*; Lord Derby had to wait until 1787 when he won with *Sir Peter Teazle*, who was the best of the early winners. Derby Day has always been a crowd-puller, as shown in Frith's famous painting. There have been many notable years, such as the 'Dirty Derby' of 1844 when the winning horse was revealed to be a four-year-old,

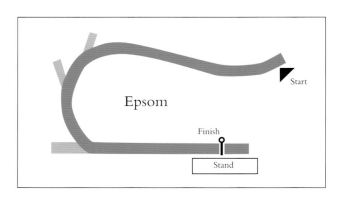

Maccabeus, rather than the three-year-old *Running Rein* he pretended to be. Another horse that year was probably six, and several were victims of deliberately bad riding or nobbling. The 1913 Derby is famous for the death of the suffragette Emily Davison, who threw herself in front of the King's horse, *Anmer*. The favourite *Craganour* was first past the post but was disqualified for bumping, and the race went to *Aboyeur*, a 100-1 outsider, who was later sold to Russia and died in the Revolution. More recent favourite Derby winners include the diminutive *Hyperion*, 1933, whose statue can be seen outside The Jockey Club, and Sir Gordon Richard's first Derby win after 27 attempts, on *Pinza* in 1953. *Shergar* won in 1981 by ten lengths, the longest margin in the race's history to date.

Shergar winning the Derby in 1981 (George Selwyn)

Various items celebrating winners of the Derby Silver model of a horse, 1896, mounted on a later plinth and inscribed in commemoration of Arctic Prince's 1951 win. **Loan: Mr W. Ryan**; *Plate worn by Ocean Swell while winning the 1944 Derby.* **Gift: Mr N. Reed-Herbert**; *Racing plate and portrait of Persimmon, winner in 1896.* **Gift: Mrs R. Hutchison**; *Cigarette box owned by Herbert Otto Madden, champion jockey in 1898, 1901, 1903 and 1904, who won the 1898 Derby on Jeddah at 100/1. His father rode the great Kincsem in most of her races.* **Gift: The Friends of the National Horseracing Museum**; *Souvenir pin of the 1876 Derby, won by Kisber.* **Gift: The Newmarket Gallery**; *Earthenware mug carrying the names of all the Derby winners up to 1876, manufactured by Lloyd & Co.* **Loan: Mr R. Pickersgill**; *Viewing Box with moveable print of 'Going to Epsom Races' by Henry Alken.* **Gift: The Friends of the National Horseracing Museum**; *Commemorative dish depicting Mahmoud, winner in 1936.* **Gift: Mr M. Beard**

St. Leger

First Race:	1776
Usual Location:	Doncaster, Yorkshire
Current Distance:	1 mile 6 furlongs 127 yards
Age:	3 year olds of both sexes but excluding Geldings
Weight:	Colts 9 stone, Fillies 8st 11lb

Spode plate celebrating the 1970 St. Leger
Gift: Mr D. Yates

The St. Leger is the oldest of the Classic races, and was first run on Cantley Common, Doncaster, being won by the 2nd Marquis of Rockingham's filly *Alabaculia*. In 1778 the race was named after Lt. Gen Anthony St. Leger, a popular local sportsman, and the race was moved to Town Moor, Doncaster.

The St. Leger broke decisively with the tradition of horses aged five and over running races over several heats and long distances. By the 19th century it had become a major social event – in 1806 bets of over a million guineas had been laid by July. Unsurprisingly, dodgy results abounded. In 1813 there were ten false starts, and in 1819 the race was rerun when *Antonio* won at 33/1 leaving five horses – including the favourite – still at the start. In the end the rerun itself was ruled out of order and the original result

The Finish of the St. Leger, 1813 by Clifton Thomson (1775-1828)

The painting shows all 17 entrants in the race, which, after ten false starts, was won by the chestnut filly Altisidora by 'half a head'. She was owned by Mr Richard Watt and ridden by John Jackson.
Anonymous Loan

stood. *Theodore* won in 1822, at 200-1, despite being desperately lame before the race. In 1825 pigeons were used to convey news of the result – a win by *Memnon* – to London.

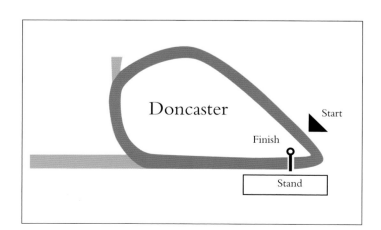

Doncaster

Start

Finish

Stand

The Oaks

First Race: 1779
Usual Location: Epsom Downs, Surrey
Current Distance: 1 mile 4 furlongs
Age: 3 year old Fillies
Weight: 9 stone

The Oaks was inaugurated three years after the first St. Leger. It was founded by the 12th Earl of Derby and named after his Epsom house. He won the first Oaks with *Bridget*. Although the Oaks is a Fillies' classic, they can also run in the Derby, but rarely do so today as the races are run on successive days. However *Eleanor* won the Derby for Sir Charles Bunbury in 1801 and went on to win the Oaks the very next day. Others to win both races were *Blink Bonny* (1857), *Signorinetta* (1908) and *Fifinella* (1916),whose races were at Newmarket due to the War.

*Wooden sculpture of Noblesse
(won in 1963)
by Jan Zolcik*
Bequest: Mrs P. G. Margetts

It is far more common for winners of the Oaks to go on to win the St. Leger and 17 have done so. One was *Pretty Polly*; she won the 1904 Oaks at the shortest odds ever returned in a Classic, of 100 – 8 on and was so good she was even 5 – 2 on to beat the colts at Doncaster.

*The mounted foot of Canterbury Pilgrim,
winner in 1896*
Gift: Mrs P. Hastings

*Christmas card commemorating
Carrozza's 1957 win*
Gift: Mrs F. Thompson

The 2000 Guineas

First Race: 1809
Usual Location: Rowley Mile Racecourse, Newmarket
Current Distance: 1 mile
Age: 3 year olds of both sexes but excluding Geldings
Weight: Colts carry 9 stone, Fillies 8 stone 9lb

Cigarette advert - Ormonde 1886,
Sculpture of Royal Palace by John Skeaping 1967
and a Racing plate worn by Shotover 1882

The name of this race derives from the fact that a prize of 2000 Guineas was originally guaranteed, irrespective of the number of subscribers. The inaugural race was won by *Wizard*, belonging to the Yorkshireman Christopher Wilson who was for many years the senior member of the Jockey Club. The 2000 Guineas soon became established as the best pointer for the Derby. The first horse to complete the double was *Smolensko* in 1813. Perhaps the finest race in recent times was in 1971, when *Brigadier Gerard* beat *Mill Reef* into second place, ridden by Joe Mercer. Both horses were true champions, a rare event in a single year.

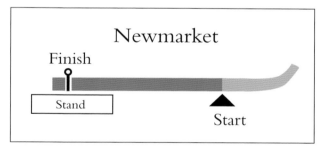

Newmarket

Finish

Stand

Start

The 1000 Guineas

First Race: 1814
Usual Location: Rowley Mile
                     Newmarket
Current Distance: 1 mile
Age: 3 year old Fillies
Weight: 9 stone

The first 1000 Guineas was also won by a horse belonging to Christopher Wilson, *Charlotte*. Until recently it was usually run two days after the 2000 Guineas, and four Fillies, *Crucifix* (1840), *Formosa* (1868), *Pilgrimage* (1878) and *Sceptre* (1902) have won both races in their year.

Mounted foot of Scuttle 1928,
Framed tail hair from Pretty Polly 1904
and the Mounted foot of Galeottia 1895

The Triple Crown

The five Classic races - the 1000 Guineas, 2000 Guineas, the Derby, the Oaks and the St. Leger - were not designed as a series, but together they have come to be regarded as the supreme test for the thoroughbred. For a colt to win the Triple Crown - 2000 Guineas, the Derby and St. Leger - he must demonstrate his pre-eminence amongst three-year-olds on Newmarket's straight mile in the Spring, around Epsom's switchback mile and a half in June, and again over the extended mile and three-quarters of Doncaster's galloping course in September. Three Triple Crown winners - *Pommern, Gay Crusader* and *Gainsborough* - did not have to show so much adaptability, since their races were all run at Newmarket due to the First World War. That leaves 12 other champions between *West Australian* (in 1853) and *Nijinsky* (in 1970) who achieved the feat the hard way.

West Australian
Print by A. F. de Prades
Loan: Mr P. Dalton White

Nijinsky
Painting of Nijinsky by Raoul Millais
Gift: Raoul Millais

Items commemorating other winners of the Triple Crown

Painting of Sceptre by Emil Adam
Gift: The Friends of the National Horseracing Museum

The Fillies' Triple Crown

Fillies which win the 1000 Guineas, Oaks and St. Leger are regarded as having won the fillies' equivalent of The Triple Crown. Nine have achieved this feat from *Formosa* in 1868 to *Oh So Sharp* in 1985. *Formosa* had won a fourth classic when she dead-heated with *Moslem* in the 2000 Guineas, and the great *Sceptre* went one better by winning that race outright. The idea of Classic Races has proved enduring and has been copied by nearly all other racing countries. Nevertheless Triple Crown winners are becoming a very rare phenomena, partly due to the sheer number of horses in training. Perhaps more relevant is the fact that horses are increasingly specialised, particularly with regard to distance. Until the First World War, Classic winners usually ran in the next season's long-distance Cup races. Today, however, the Prix de l'Arc de Triomphe at Longchamps (founded 1920) and the King George VI and Queen Elizabeth Stakes at Ascot (1951) are the preferred tests for Classic winners from different countries and of different ages.

Mounted Foot of Sceptre.
Sceptre, who won the fillies' Triple Crown and the 2000
Guineas in 1902, was a bay mare by Persimmon out of
Ornament. Her lad named his daughter after her.
Loan: Estate of the late Major David Gibson

Cadeaux Genereux
by Trevor Jones

THE THOROUGHBRED HORSE

Over 100,000 thoroughbred foals are born world-wide each year. Astonishingly, all can trace their ancestry back, father to father, to one of three imported horses – the *Godolphin Arabian*, the *Byerley Turk* or the *Darley Arabian*.

English Racehorse (c. 1690)
by John Baptist Closterman (d. 1713)
The racehorse in this painting clearly has less
Eastern blood than later thoroughbreds. He is standing with his
jockey in a landscape below Haddon Hall in Derbyshire.
Gift: The Friends of the National
Horseracing Museum

The crucial years for the development of the thoroughbred were the late 17th century to about 1750, during which period some 150 stallions were imported from the Middle East with coherent pedigrees developed in the desert over the centuries. Native breeds were more or less 'mongrels', despite the influence of earlier imports, which failed to breed true, so even though the fresh importations were usually slower they had a huge influence. They were mated with mares bought, in smaller numbers, from the same source, or more commonly with those drawn from 'running strains' already existing in England. The number of foundation mares whose descendants appear in the General Stud Book is estimated at just 78, and some of these are probably duplicated due to confusion over names.

The imported stallions were Arabians, Barbs or Turks, depending upon their supposed origin, prefixed with the name of their current owner. Changes of name as the stallions were sold and resold, combined with poorly maintained stud records, have led to great confusion in attempting to trace the development of the thoroughbred. Adding to the muddle, many horses shared the same name, often at the same time. Nevertheless, the importance of the three founding fathers of the turf, the *Godolphin Arabian*, the *Byerley Turk* and the *Darley Arabian*, is a matter of record.

The *Godolphin Arabian*, foaled in about 1724, was said to have been found pulling a Paris watercart, but was probably exported from Yemen via Syria to the stud of the Bey of Tunis before being given to Louis XV in 1730. Like the other two, he did not race himself, and was in fact unprolific as a stallion. However, the quality of his descendants was outstanding. As a result of his mating with *Roxana*, he produced the best racehorse of the day, *Lath*. Next year *Roxana* died foaling *Cade*, who sired *Matchem* from whom all *Godolphin* line horses descend. His direct line is now overshadowed by the *Darley Arabian* line through *Eclipse*, and a descendant of his has not won the Derby since *Santa Claus* in 1964.

The *Byerley Turk* (foaled about

Fathers of the Turf by John Beer
Gift: Captain M. Lemos

The Godolphin Arabian
Gift: The Friends of the National Horseracing Museum

1680), through *Herod*, was responsible for the line which includes *The Tetrarch* and the recent Derby winners *Blakeney* and *Dr Devious*. *Herod*, foaled in 1758, was described by a contemporary as 'a stallion inferior to none' and indeed was leading sire eight times. The most important of his progeny was *Highflyer* – he and his sons were champion stallions 23 times in 25 years. However, despite its influence at the time, the *Herod / Highflyer* line is now far less influential than that of the *Darley Arabian*.

Herod

Flying Childers
Anonymous loans

The *Darley Arabian* (foaled about 1700) was sent to England from the Near East at the age of four. He sired the full brothers *Flying Childers* and *Bartlett's Childers*, the former a great racehorse and the latter important for the continuation of the line. Well over 80% of modern racehorses can trace their descent to *Bartlett's Childers'* great grandson, *Eclipse*, many of them through the great American stallion *Northern Dancer*.

Eclipse was foaled in 1764, the year of the great eclipse of the sun. He won 18 races, and was never stretched or headed in any of them – indeed, his jockeys had a problem holding him at all. Few owners were willing to risk their horses against him, and eight of his races were 'walkovers'.

Northern Dancer (foaled 1961)
Pastel by Klaus Phillips
Loan: Private Collection

Portrait of Eclipse, by J.N. Sartorius
Anonymous Loan

Eclipse first raced when he was five years old, and easily won the first heat of his first public race, at Epsom in May 1769. An Irish gambler named O'Kelly correctly predicted the placings of the next heat with the bet '*Eclipse* first, the rest nowhere' – *Eclipse* finished before the other runners were even at the distance post, 240 yards before the winning post, which under the rules meant they could not be placed. *Eclipse* retired to stud in 1771 and sired three early Derby winners. However, fine stallion that he was, he was never actually champion due to competition from *Herod* and his stock.

As well as the three founding fathers, others, such as the *Curwen Bay Barb, Leedes Arabian* and both the *Darcy Yellow* and *White Turks*, made important contributions although their direct lines have not survived to modern times.

As early as 1727 John Cheney published a calendar of races run that year in which he included, with difficulty, a large number of pedigrees. The first General Stud Book, collating the then known records back to the early days, was produced by James Weatherby in 1791. In it he effectively defined thoroughbreds as horses which had descended from certain mares. Nevertheless horses which were excluded could still be raced in this country, as they still can be today.

Thanks to its adaptability, the thoroughbred altered as the emphasis in racing changed from endurance tests for mature horses. Admiral Rous estimated that they got larger by an inch every 25 years, and they certainly got faster over shorter distances and matured earlier.

Skeleton of Eclipse
After his death in 1789, Eclipse was dissected by Charles Vial de Sainbel, Professor of the Veterinary College of London, in order to try to find the secret to his phenomenal success. It has been suggested that he had great leverage from his hind legs, and powerful lungs Sainbel proved he had a huge heart to pump oxygen round the body effectively.
Loan: The Royal Veterinary College

After the mid-19th century horses which had been bred abroad began to be imported into England. They were almost wholly bred from English stock, sometimes exported several generations earlier. One, the French-bred *Gladiateur*, astounded the English by winning the Triple Crown in 1865. He finished his career by winning the Grand Prix de l'Empereur in Paris and retired to stud at a fee of 100 guineas, but was a total disappointment as a sire.

Kincsem, foaled in Hungary in 1874, one of the greatest fillies of the 19th century, had an English import as a sire. She raced for four seasons and was unbeaten in 54 races all over Europe, but only came to Britain once, when she won the Goodwood Cup. She apparently whinnied with pleasure whenever she saw a train, her normal method of transport around Europe. Her tally for an unbeaten horse has never been approached anywhere before or since, and as good a judge as George Lambton voted her the best racehorse of either sex ever foaled. Sadly, she died at only 13 but still had time to found an enduring family through her three daughters.

Gladiateur's tail
Loan: Jockey Club Estates Ltd.

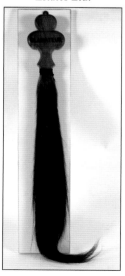

Kincsem (1874)
Gift: The Friends of the Museum

Horseracing enjoyed a second golden age between 1875 and the Great War. Major strides were made on all fronts, not least with the thoroughbred itself. Appropriately, *Galopin* (sire of the great *St. Simon* who was to become the most influential stallion since *Eclipse*), won the Derby as the era began. Five years later, *Hermit*, winner of the 1867 Derby, became the Champion Sire for the first of 7 consecutive years.

The early horses were stayers which varied primarily in terms of speed. However, as priorities changed horses were bred to specialise as either sprinters or stayers. Nowadays only the best horses can transcend such limitations.

Following the reign of *Hermit* as Champion stallion came the even more illustrious nine years of *St. Simon*. Their joint influence was huge. However their fame was challenged on the course by the likes of the Triple Crown winners *Isinglass* and *Ormonde*, and on the course and at stud by *Persimmon*. *Persimmon's* daughter *Sceptre* was one of The Turf's all time heroines, along with her contemporary, *Pretty Polly*, who won 22 of her 24 races. Sadly they never met in a race but both founded families which have lasted to this day.

However times change in bloodstock breeding and the

Hermit (foaled 1864), photograph taken in 1890, the year of his death.
Gift: Turf Newspapers

declining *St. Simon* and *Herod* lines were only saved by imports. The five best horses to have run in Britain since the war must include S*ea Bird II* and *Ribot*, and probably *Nijinsky* and *Mill Reef*, all of whom were bred abroad. American thoroughbreds were not warmly welcomed when they came to Britain, partly because their ancestry could not always be traced accurately to English stock. In reaction, the 1913 'Jersey Act' excluded horses and mares from the General Stud Book which could not trace their ancestry back to others in the book "without flaw". However, the need to strengthen British horses with fresh blood led to relaxation of this rule in 1948 and again in 1969.

The UK breeding industry has had its triumphs too: for instance wartime champions *Hurry On* and *Gainsborough*; *Pharos* and *Fairway* in the 20s, *Windsor Lad* and *Bahram* in the 30s, and then *Pinza, Meld, Petite Etoile* and *Brigadier Gerard* in the years after the war. Nowadays champions, wherever foaled, are invariably a mixture of various international bloodlines.

In the 19th century, the aristocracy owned the large studs. Some, like the Derbys at Knowsley and Stanley House and the Rothschilds and then Roseberys at Mentmore, survived until after the Second War. However, nowadays, racehorse breeding, like the horses themselves, is an international business. The major owner/breeders such as the Maktoum brothers, Prince Khalid Abdullah, HH The Aga Khan and Robert Sangster, have international breeding and racing programmes. Yet the bulk of thoroughbreds are bred in smaller, usually commercial studs. Sales ring potential is paramount to such breeders. Auctions of yearling thoroughbreds take place worldwide, notably at Keeneland in the US, Ireland, Australia and in France, and of course at Tattersalls in Newmarket as well as at Doncaster.

St. Simon (foaled 1881) Photograph taken from a glass negative
Gift: Turf Newspapers

Pretty Polly by Alfred C Havell
Gift: Macdonald-Buchanan Family Charitable Trust

The Paddock at Tattersalls by Isaac Cullin (working 1875-1920)
All the individuals in the painting, including the Prince of Wales and the auctioneer Richard Tattersall, can be identified
Loan: Private Collection

RACEHORSE NAMES

Racehorses' names must be registered with Weatherbys, who receive about 12,000 new applications each year. The names are often clever combinations of the horse's sire and dam, as for example Her Majesty the Queen's horse *RASH GIFT*, by *CADEAUX GENEREUX* out of *NETTLE*.

The name must follow certain rules:

• It must be no more than 18 characters long (including spaces).

• Initials must be spelled out, for example 'jay-ess-bee' rather than 'JSB'.

• It must be in good taste - if in doubt, Weatherbys refers to a dictionary of slang.

• It must not appear on the list of 250,000 Registered Names
This list includes -
  All horses for a period after their recorded death or they cease to be recorded in training or at stud, from the year of their birth.
  All Classic winners and winners of the Ascot Gold Cup, the King George VI and Queen Elizabeth Diamond Stakes, Grand National together with some other races of international importance such as the Cheltenham Gold Cup.

• It must not appear on the International List of Protected Names, which includes celebrated names such as *ARKLE*.

A name may be forbidden in this country but permitted elsewhere, so that a horse may share a name with one foaled abroad. A horse bred outside the British Isles is given a code for its country after its name, for example *Nijinski (CAN)*, so that the two horses can still be differentiated.

Tattersalls was founded by Mr Richard Tattersall, who leased land at Hyde Park Corner in 1766. At the time, there were adjoining fields which could be used to exercise horses, and Tattersall built stables, kennels and stands for the sale of carriages. The twice-weekly sales became highly successful, and by 1785 Tattersalls covered 15 acres. Sales were conducted in Newmarket from the end of the 18th century and for a long time the company's premier yearling sale was at Doncaster. Until about 1860 those at Newmarket took place outside the Jockey Club Rooms, but in 1870 they moved to near their present site. All Tattersalls British sales are now held here, and in 1997 they sold horses for £125 million, of which nearly £60 million related to yearlings. Breeding is an inexact science. An expensive horse with an amazing pedigree may prove to be quite useless on the course - *Snaafi Dancer* (bought as a yearling for $10.2m in 1983) is a famous example. Fortunately, the opposite is also true now and again and champions like *Pinza* and *Brigadier Gerard* can have relatively humble backgrounds.

Lammtarra and Walter Swinburn being congratulated by Sheikh Mohammed, after their Derby win in 1995 (George Selwyn)

OWNERS AND BREEDERS

As the numbers and types of races in Britain have changed according to economic, social and legislative factors, so the predominant type of owner has altered. From the 1550s until the 1680s important race meetings were timed to coincide with the movements of the Court around the country, so the main owners were the royal family and their courtiers. At the local and municipal meetings, the owners were mostly the major local families.

These owners did not usually breed their horses. Perhaps eighty percent of thoroughbreds were produced by studs located around the Vale of York until the 18th century and many of these studs were at least partially commercial operations, providing stock for others to race at Newmarket and elsewhere.

After 1685, ownership and breeding spread beyond the aristocracy as the sport became a national passion. However, high-class breeding and racing still centred on Newmarket and in Yorkshire. Many other race meetings were small, disorganised and corrupt, so in 1740 an Act of Parliament banned races worth under £50. Once again, the pendulum swung back towards the aristocracy, in particular now to owners who bred their own stock on their estates. This relatively small circle sold their horses to each other, often for very large sums, and expected to bet lucratively on them.

Lord Falmouth

The Eaton Stud

Mentmore

Typical of the owner-breeders were the 1st Earl Grosvenor (1731-1802, Eaton Stud), Lord Falmouth (1819-1889, Mereworth Castle), and Baron Meyer de Rothschild (1818 - 1874, Mentmore).

Horses which have won a Classic race are worth more at stud than on the racecourse. However, the eventual success of a stud rests on mares who establish families which produce Classic and other great winners. Thus the 3rd Duke of Grafton (1735-1811) had an important effect on the evolution of the thoroughbred through his purchase of *Julia*, who established an impressive family of champion stallions and brood mares. His son the 4th Duke (1760 - 1844) was able to exploit these lines in partnership with his trainer Robert Robson. He achieved 20 Classic wins, including 19 with horses that he had bred, many with the jockeys Francis Buckle or John Day in the saddle.

The grip of the owner-breeder was relaxed firstly in the 1830s, and again after 1870 when agricultural decline ate into the fortunes of landowners. However, owner-breeders such as the Dukes of Westminster, the Duke of Portland and the Earls of Rosebery and newcomers like the 2nd Viscount Astor and Lord Woolavington maintained their influence.

The 1st Duke of Westminster (1825-1899) was the only man to breed and own two Triple Crown winners; *Ormonde* and *Flying Fox*. His son was less knowledgable or interested and only achieved two Classic wins.

The 6th Duke of Portland (1857-1943) revived his family's Welbeck Stud when he inherited his title in 1879. *St. Simon*, whom he purchased on the advice of his trainer Mat Dawson, was never beaten and became one of the greatest sires in the history of British breeding.

The 5th Earl of Rosebery (1847 - 1929), who was sent down from Oxford for owning a racehorse, inherited the Mentmore Stud through his wife Hannah, the heiress of Baron Rothschild. Like the 3rd Duke of Grafton, the 2nd Marquis of Rockingham, the 14th Earl of Derby and Lord Palmerston, the Earl combined his racing interests with duties as Prime Minister. His son, the 6th Earl, was an outstanding athlete, cricketer, golfer and polo player and also held important public offices outside the racing world. Nevertheless he managed to continue his father's success as an owner-breeder. His best horse was *Blue Peter* who had won the 1939 2000 Guineas and Derby before the outbreak of war deprived him of his chance of the Triple Crown.

Blue Peter (foaled 1936)
Blue Peter was owned by the 6th Earl of Rosebery and trained by Jack Jarvis. He won the 2000 Guineas, Derby and Eclipse Stakes but the St. Leger was abandoned when war broke out
Gift: Mrs M. Ponder

Oxygen
Loan: The Duke of Grafton

Two other owners-breeder, Lord Astor and Lord Woolavington, typify a new type of owner, crudely characterised as 'new money'. Lord Astor (1879 - 1952) inherited vast wealth from his New York family. He founded the Cliveden Stud in 1916 and bred 12 Classic winners (although the last won a sixth Oaks after his death for his son). Strangely, he never won the Derby although his horses were second five times. James Buchanan (1849-1935) (created Lord Woolavington) built up his own fortune in the distillery business and invested wisely in horses, particularly with *Epsom Lad* and *Hurry On*. He bred his Derby winners *Captain Cuttle* and *Coronach*. Other 'new money' owners who made an impact in racing were Sir J. Blundell Maple, who made his fortune in the furniture business, W. M. G. Singer, son of the sewing-machine millionaire, and Walter Raphael, a London financier.

*Portrait of George Fordham
in the colours of
Comte Frederic de Lagrange*
Purchase

From the 1860s an international dimension entered ownership. Count de Lagrange, an owner-breeder based in France, owned *Gladiateur* who won the Triple Crown and became nicknamed 'The Avenger of Waterloo'. Later American owners and money from the Empire became important, the latter principally via the Joel family, the Wernhers and Mr A. W. Cox.

Derby scarf produced to commemorate Captain Cuttle's win
Loan: Mr W. Jardine

Racing plate worn by Lemberg in the 1910 Derby
Gift: Mr A. S. Cox

Mr Alfred W. Cox (1857-1919) had been sent to Australia in disgrace, but on the way won a share in a derelict sheep farm in a game of poker. At the farm he spotted a glint in the dust; the farm became the famous Broken Hill silver mines and Cox returned to England ten years later with a huge fortune. Racing under the name 'Mr Fairie' he bred *Galicia*, the brood mare who in turn bred *Bayardo* and *Lemberg*. He also bred and owned *Gay Crusader* who won the Triple Crown in 1917.

The fortunes of J. B. 'Jack' Joel (1862-1940) came from South African diamond mines and other large businesses. He began racing around 1900. *Sunstar* won the 2000 Guineas and the Derby for him in 1911, and his second Derby came a decade later with *Humorist*. His success with breeding and racing horses was due to hard work and study, but also an exceptionally good 20-year relationship with his trainer Charles Morton. His results were moderate after Morton retired.

His Royal Highness The Prince of Wales with Mr J.B. Joel prior to 'Humorist's' Derby win 1921. A young Jim Joel is between them
Gift: Mr H. J. Joel

Jack Joel's brother Mr S. B. 'Solly' Joel shared his mining and racing interests and owned *Pommern*, the 1915 Triple Crown winner, while Jack's son Mr Jim Joel inherited a fortune and his Childwick Bury Stud which he revitalised. *Royal Palace* won the Derby and 2000 Guineas for him in 1967. A generous and popular man, he was one of the original benefactors of this Museum.

Two world wars and increasing tax levels led to many owners selling up. The established owner/breeders had to share their successes with newcomers such as the Aga Khan and Sir Victor Sassoon.

The Aga Khan III (1877-1957) almost dominated racing in the 1930s, when he had at least two runners in many big races. He approached racing as a mentally stimulating business which he studied at length before asking George Lambton to help him purchase horses to place with the trainer R. C. Dawson. By his third season as an owner in Britain he had won the 2000 Guineas with *Diophon* and become leading owner. By the 30s his empire of horses and studs was the largest to date in the history of the British turf. Mares such as *Mumtaz Mahal* and *Friar's Daughter* bred other important Classic winners. *Friar's Daughter's* son *Bahram*, the Triple Crown winner, is probably the Aga Khan's best-

The Aga Khan III leading in 'Bahram' with F. Fox after the 1935 Derby
The Triple Crown winner Bahram was so loved by his lad that he named his children Barbara, Barnaby etc after the horse

remembered horse. He sold *Bahram* and *Mahmoud* (who won the Derby in 1936) to the USA early in the war. This exodus continued after the war ended and played a large part in the later success of horses bred in Kentucky especially via *Nasrullah*.

Sir Victor Sassoon (1881 - 1961) invested in racing on nearly the same scale as the Aga Khan but took far longer to achieve the same sort of results. His first Classic victory was with *Exhibitionnist*, who won first the 1000 Guineas and then the Oaks in 1937. *Pinza*, bred by the great trainer Fred Darling, won the Derby for him in 1953; he won another three Derbys and nine Classics in all. Unlike the Aga Khan, Sir Victor refused big offers from abroad for his stallions. It would have been better for the European thoroughbred if it had been the other way around as only *Crepello* of his four Derby winners had much success as a stallion.

After the Second World War, top races were increasingly won by horses owned by non-residents, many of whom were Americans who were using American bloodstock trained here or in Ireland. *Sir Ivor, Nijinsky, Mill Reef, Roberto, Vaguely Noble* and *Grundy* were all foreign-owned, even if the last two were bred here. Only Lord Howard de Walden, Lord Weinstock, his father-in-law Sir Michael Sobell and Mr Louis Freedman have had consistent top level success as British rather than international owner/breeders in recent years.

Today over 10,000 people own all or part of a horse and there are about 13,000 horses in training at any one time. A few international owner/breeders with large strings dominate the scene: the Maktoum brothers, Khalid Abdullah, Robert Sangster, the Aga Khan and, on a slightly smaller scale, Fahd Salman.

The impact of the Maktoum family on British racing has been enormous since the early 1980s. As well as horses in training, they own several studs, notably the Dalham Hall, Shadwell and Gainsborough Studs, as well as others in Canada, Ireland, France and the USA.

Sheikh Mohammed's first Classic winner came in 1985 when *Oh So Sharp* won the Fillies Triple Crown. His elder brother Maktoum Al-Maktoum won the 1982 St. Leger with *Touching Wood*, and another brother Hamdam Al-Maktoum had success with the brilliant *Nashwan*, the 1989 2000 Guineas and Derby winner. Since then many Classic winners have had a Maktoum interest, notably the outstanding *Lammtarra* (Derby 1995) who was unbeaten in 1994 and 1995, ending with a win in the Arc de Triomphe. Some feel that the Maktoum family has distorted the market through their sheer buying power, whilst others recognise the positive impact of their investment in racing. No owners before have had so many horses in training, leading to significant local employment in the industry. In any case they face significant competition from the others mentioned, who have already shared eight Derbys between them.

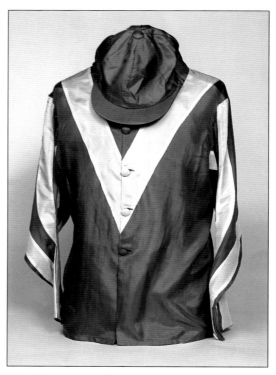

Silks worn in all three of Lammtarra's 1995
victories as a three year old
Gift: Godolphin Management Company Ltd

The Blackbushe Car Auction Graduation Stakes at Kempton Park in 1987 (Trevor Jones)

As well as these dominant players, there are increasing numbers of smaller owners and shared horses via partnerships, syndicates and clubs. Racing is working hard to dispel the image of racehorse ownership as the sole province of the super-rich. However, few owners expect to live on their winnings, and must bear in mind that it costs about £15,000 a year to keep a horse in training, with veterinary, farriery, transport, insurance and other expenses on top.

The ownership of each horse in a race is indicated by the colours worn by the jockey. In 1762 the Jockey Club produced a list of 19 colours 'for the greater convenience of distinguishing the horses in running and also for the prevention of disputes arising from not knowing the colours worn by each rider.'

Today's colour chart

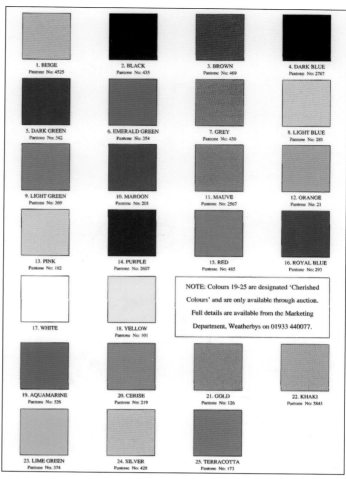

The patterns that an owner must choose for his or her silks
Courtesy of Weatherbys

Of the original list, only two have lasted: the *Devonshire Straw* and the *Grosvenor Orange* (the latter is now Yellow in the Westminster version of the colours). A few colours have been held by the same family for so long that they too have become historical tones, for example Lord Howard de Walden's '*apricot*'. The Duke of Cumberland's '*purple*' is clearly the basis for the Royal colours. Caps were not mentioned in 1762 but paintings show that they were usually black rather than in the same colour as the body.

Today a new owner must choose from a selection of 18 basic colours and a series of patterns (quartering, spots etc). All single colours have been taken up, although Weatherbys very occasionally auctions new ones or simple combinations which sell for many thousands of pounds.

Henry Cecil (Trevor Jones)

TRAINERS

In the 17th and 18th centuries, although major owners had separate establishments for their racehorses, the names of the training grooms in charge of them are largely unrecorded. However they often appear in equine portraits, sometimes holding the horse by the reins while it is rubbed down by a stable lad or admiring their handywork from the back of a hack.

Sketch by Samuel Alken Junior (1784-1825)
Gift: Mrs T. Nickalls

It was considered self-evident that a light horse would race faster, so great efforts were made to get rid of surplus flesh. Horses were sweated, purged and galloped in heavy clothing, so that when they emerged for a race they looked like toast racks. They were kept heavily rugged in heated, non-ventilated stables, and carefully kept out of draughts. It is said that only an artist of the calibre of Stubbs could persuade an owner to allow a horse to pose for him 'naked'.

Matilda (1824) by J.F. Herring Senior
Gift: Simon Gibson Esq in memory of Lord Glanely

The greatest trainer at the beginning of the 19th century was Robert Robson (1765-1838) who was notably gentle with his horses. He won the Derby with *Waxy* in 1793 before moving to Newmarket and training six more Derby winners. He won the 1000 Guineas eight times for the 4th Duke of Grafton, the 2000 Guineas five times and the Oaks nine (Robson had no St. Leger winners because southern horses rarely went north). Lord Grosvenor was another important owner for Robson, who in some ways bridged the gap between the training grooms who worked for a single owner and public trainers who accepted horses from a number of different owners.

The first great truly public trainer was John Scott (1794 – 1871) of Whitewall, in Malton, Yorkshire, who trained the winners of 41 classic races including the first ever Triple Crown winner, *West Australian*. His owners included the Hon Edward Petre, Mr John Bowes, the Marquis of Westminster and the Earls of Derby and Chesterfield. At first his brother William was stable jockey, but after he died of drink Frank Butler, Nat Flatman and others rode regularly for him.

From the 1870s, the most consistently successful stable in England was that of Mathew Dawson (1820-1898). He set up his public yard in 1866, first in St. Marys Square and then at Heath House in Newmarket. His first major patron was Lord Falmouth for whom he won 12 Classics, mostly with his retained jockey Fred Archer. Later important owners were the Duke of Portland and Lord Rosebery.

Mathew Dawson
Photograph from Racing Illustrated

Mathew Dawson's brother Thomas (1809-1880), who trained at Middleham, was the first trainer in the north to abandon the heavy sweating regime, known slightly sarcastically as 'Yorkshire Sweats' south of the Trent, beginning in the 1840s. Derision turned to duplication when it was realised that the horses became better-tempered and less likely to break down due to leg injuries.

John Porter of Kingsclere (1838-1922) was Mathew Dawson's great rival at the end of the 19th century, winning over 1000 races, of which seven were Derbys. Kingsclere was built by Sir Joseph Hawley (1814-1875) for whom he won the Derby and St. Leger to add to three Derbys already in the bag. Porter bought the yard himself when Sir Joseph died, and enjoyed the patronage of a string of wealthy owners including the newly-created Duke of Westminster and the Prince of Wales. He was unique in training three Triple Crown winners – *Ormonde, Common* and *Flying Fox*.

The Kingsclere stables
Photograph from Racing Illustrated

The profession of training racehorses was slowly beginning to become respectable. George Lambton (1860 –

The Hon George Lambton
Photograph from Racing Illustrated

1945) was the fifth son of the 2nd Earl of Durham. A successful amateur jockey, he turned to training as the result of a fall. He became private trainer to the 16th Earl of Derby in 1893, and took control of the Earl's Bedford Lodge stables, moving with him to Stanley House in 1903. Lambton was particularly concerned with the American 'import' of doping to win, and persuaded the Jockey Club of its effect with a practical demonstration; it was made an offence the following year (doping to lose had always been a crime). He continued to work for the next Lord Derby in various roles, winning the Derby and St. Leger for him with *Hyperion* in 1933. This was his 13th and last Classic win, but he continued to train for other owners until two days before he died, in 1945. His autobiography, *Men and Horses I Have Known*, is a delight.

Fred Darling (1884 - 1953) began training in 1907 and took over his father's Beckhampton stable in 1913. His best horse was perhaps *Hurry On*, who won all his six races including the St. Leger. *Hurry On's* son *Captain Cuttle* won the Derby for him in 1922. In all he trained 19 winners of Classic races, of which 7 were Derbys. He owned as well as trained *Pont l'Eveque*, who won the Derby for him in 1940. After his retirement, Darling devoted himself to his stud where he bred *Pinza* - he died three days after *Pinza* (owned by Sir Victor Sassoon) won the Derby in 1953. It is said only his hope of the horse's triumph kept him alive beyond expectation.

*Bronze of Nijinsky
by Launcelot Jones*
Loan: L. Jones

Alec Taylor (1862-1943), 'The Wizard of Manton', was champion trainer 12 times, with 21 Classics to his credit, including the Triple Crown winners *Gay Crusader* and *Gainsborough*. Frank Butters (1877-1957) must also be mentioned. A member of the linked Butters and Waugh racing dynasties, he returned to Britain aged nearly 50 as private trainer to the 17th Earl of Derby at Stanley House, and was leading trainer by the end of his first season there. When in 1930 George Lambton resumed control at Stanley House, Butters opened a public stable at Fitzroy House and trained for owners such as the Aga Khan, including his Triple Crown winner *Bahram*. By the time he retired in 1949, he had 15 Classic winners to his credit and had been champion 8 times.

Noel Murless specialised in training horses for the Classics with a great deal of success. Starting as a trainer at Hambleton, Yorkshire, in 1935, he soon acquired an impressive list of owners and really made his mark after the war. Moving first to Fred Darling's Beckhampton stables in 1947 and then to Warren Place, Newmarket in 1952, for a quarter of a century his record was highly impressive. When Gordon Richards retired as stable jockey in 1954, he was replaced by Lester Piggott. This partnership, one of the most successful in racing history, lasted 12 seasons and included Classic wins with *Crepello, Carrozza, Petite Etoile, St. Paddy* and *Aurelius*. Noel Murless retired in 1976 and was knighted the following year.

Not all trainers specialise either on the flat or in National Hunt - Vincent O'Brien reached the top in both. His major successes between 1948 and 1955 were predominantly earned under National Hunt rules but from about 1956 he concentrated on flat horses. During the next thirty years he achieved many more triumphs, particularly in the Classics, often with American-bred horses ridden by Lester Piggott. He has six Derbys under his belt, including that of *Nijinsky*, the 15th winner of the Triple Crown (1970). He was also the first man to transport horses regularly by air rather than by sea and train and even experimented with taking horses abroad for the sun in the winter, a policy now back in favour with the transfer of horses to Dubai.

There are currently about 500 licensed trainers in Britain, and a further 200 or so 'permit holders' who may only

*Henry Cecil
from the mural by
Jacquie Jones
1997*

train their own horses or those of their immediate family. Horses are trained nationwide, but there are concentrations in Newmarket (where there are about 2,500 horses in training), Lambourn in Berkshire, and Malton and Middleham, both in Yorkshire. Some trainers, such as Henry Cecil, have over two hundred horses, but most have much fewer. Architecture in yards can vary between Victorian and Edwardian traditional stables and huge, American barns, but in all successful yards horses in training are treated with a care which borders on reverence.

Henry Cecil became assistant trainer to his step-father, Captain Sir Cecil Boyd-Rochfort, and soon took over his Freemason Lodge stables in 1968. He moved into Noel Murless' yard at Warren Place when Sir Cecil retired, having married Julie Murless. His horses have won countless races (180 in 1987 alone), including the fillies' Triple Crown with *Oh So Sharp* and the Derby with *Slip Anchor, Reference Point, Commander-in-Chief* and *Oath*.

Shergar - in some ways the most famous racehorse ever - was trained by Michael Stoute (now Sir Michael). Sir Michael worked for Pat Rohan in Yorkshire, then Doug Smith and Tom Jones in Newmarket before setting up on his own in 1972. He was the first trainer in this country to win an English Classic in five consecutive seasons, from 1985. His extraordinary knack with older horses was well exemplified by the recent careers of *Singspiel* and *Pilsudski*.

SUMMER ROUTINE IN A MIXED OR FLAT RACING STABLE

5.00 am Trainer puts out list for staff, showing who rides which horse for each lot, which horses need special tack, what clothing is required, which horses' temperatures need to be taken, which horses are going racing, are to be shod/plated, and are to see the vet.

5.30 am Head Lads and Assistant Trainer unlock yard. All horses checked for problems, those which have not eaten well have their temperature checked, doubtful horses from the previous day jogged up etc.

5.45 am Stable Lads and girls start work. Each mucks out their three horses and any spares, sands and disinfects floors, put fresh litter in, hay and water all horses. The first lot (the first string of horses to go out for exercise) are tacked up. The second and third lots are fed.

6.00 am First four horses are put on the horsewalker.

6.15 am Trainer consults Assistant and Head Lad and checks any doubtful horses.

6.30 am Blacksmith checks all horses' feet. Trainer has breakfast; reads trade newspaper by 7.00 am.

6.45 am Next four horses are put on the horsewalker.

7.00 am Trainer rides/drives out with first lot, mostly horses in strong work. Those in full training will gallop seriously (work) only twice a week, with two jockeys riding out.

8.00 am Next four horses are put on the horsewalker.

8.15 am First lot come in; groomed, swum if hot, and fed.

8.30 am Second lot tacked up. These are horses which are not in serious work, either because they are backward or they have recently raced. They are in cantering or steady galloping work. Office. Entries and declarations done; post opened and answered; jockeys, horseboxes and stabling etc booked; owners rung.

9.00 am Second lot pull out. Trainer goes out with them, or off to the races. Next four horses put on horsewalker.

10.00 am Next four horses put on horsewalker.

10.15 am Second lot returns; groomed, swum if hot, and fed.

10.30 am Lads go for breakfast for half an hour

10.45 am Trainer continues in office, ringing other trainers for plans, going through races etc.

Toby Balding's Yard (Trevor Jones)

11.00 am Lads return. Third lot of horses pull out. These are mainly horses on the easy list, ie steady cantering. Stalls practice, trotting, walking, swimming etc. Horses which are backward, have just run, or are lame or off colour. Horses on Horsewalker changed agian

11.15 am Vet's routine visit to see lame horses, do any injections, endoscoping etc required. Trainer goes round with vet, and continues with office work, answering second post. Goes through tomorrow's final accepters etc. Spare lads do yards, sweep up, go round with vet, do midday hay, feed etc.

12.00 noon Last group of horses taken off horsewalker.

12.30 pm All horses fed and lads go to lunch.

1.00 pm Trainer has lunch and finishes reading the papers.

2.00 pm Trainer sleeps (unless racing)

3.00 pm Trainer does office work. Prepares next day's list and goes through races for which entries have been published today.

3.45 pm Lads return for Evening Stables. Lads muck out and groom their horses and any spares, clean headcollars etc. Vet arrives to take any routine blood tests, looks round with trainer.

4.00 pm Horses on horsewalker

5.00 pm Second group on horsewalker

5.30 pm Trainer and/or Assistant looks round evening stables, feels all legs and checks each horse – jogging up any that may be lame etc. Sorts out horses needing veterinary attention, wounds dressing, legs bandaging etc.

6.30 pm All horses fed. Trainer goes through tomorrow's list with Assistant Trainer and makes any alterations required as a result of evening stable tour.

6.40 pm End of Evening Stables

7.15 pm Trainer has supper

8.00 pm Trainer continues with office work, going through races, ringing owners etc.

Horses leave and return from races throughout the day according to where they are racing or where they are returning from. Each are accompanied by the Travelling Head Lad or Lass, who ensures that the runners are ready and that the correct owner's colours and horse's passport go with them. The horse's 'own' lad/girl will accompany the horse.

JOCKEYS

In the early days, gentlemen frequently rode their own racehorses or occasionally hired a small boy if the weights in the race required it. As racing became more organised, owners continued to put their own grooms into the saddle or employed professional jockeys.

Professional jockeys had a poor image. They were frequently unkempt and often dishonest – they could bet on horses other than their own to win, earn a lot of money by pulling a horse, and were positively encouraged to cross and jostle, often within the rules of the day. They would ride for anyone, although some received a retainer so that one trainer or owner had first call on their services.

The first nationally important jockeys were John Singleton (1732 – 1826), winner of the first St. Leger, Tom Jackson (1704 – 1766), John Pratt (1740 – 1829) and Sam Chifney (1753-1807). The first three were a credit to their profession but the latter was positively a dandy and less than honest. His early success (the Derby and four Oaks amongst other wins) was due to his use of tactics, in particular a late rush and a gentle use of the reins. However he fell out of favour after the *Escape* affair. Having sold his annuity from the Prince of Wales for a capital sum which he then spent, he died a debtor in 1807.

In contrast, Francis Buckle (1766 – 1832) was scrupulously honest. During his fifty-year career he achieved 27 Classic wins, a total only exceeded by Lester Piggott. Only 3st 13lbs when he first weighed out, he was known as the 'Pocket Hercules' and much loved for his honesty and simplicity of character. Even when racing against a horse on which he had bet a large sum, he could be counted upon to try his hardest.

James (Jem) Robinson (1793 – 1865), third in the list of Classic winning jockeys after Piggott and Buckle, learned much from watching Buckle and rode many matches against him. A surprising number of the horses he rode to victory in great races were bad-tempered, perhaps because of his harsh use of the whip.

There are many important 19th century jockeys – the Day family, Sam Chifney the younger, Nat Flatman, George Fordham, Bill Scott, the Arnull dynasty and many more – but the best remembered must be Fred Archer (1857-1886). During his lifetime he was a legend, and his immortality was already assured when, in 1886, he shot himself at his Newmarket home. He was only 29 but had been champion jockey for 13 consecutive years, a record sequence that even Gordon Richards with his 25 championships did not equal.

*Francis Buckle
by Richard Jones*
Purchase

Silks, racing saddle, whip, boots and documents owned by Francis Buckle. Buckle farmed near Peterborough and rode to Newmarket for trials with his racing saddle strapped across his back. The photograph shows the objects shortly after they had been acquired at auction from descendants, and before conservation. The colours are those of Lord Grosvenor.
Purchase

*Nat Flatman
by Harry Hall*
**Gift: The Friends of the
National Horseracing Museum**

*Fred Archer outside Falmouth House,
Newmarket, 1885
Photograph by Mr H. R. Sherbourne*
Loan: Mrs M. Harris

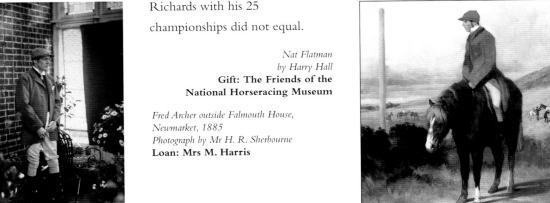

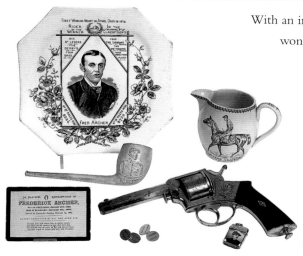

Selection of memorabilia relating to Fred Archer, including the revolver with which he took his own life

Fred Archer on Ormonde by A. Wheeler (1815 - 1932)
Gift: Mr E. George

Steve Donoghue 1924
by W. Smithson Broadhead
Gift: The Friends of the National Horseracing Museum

With an intuitive understanding of horses and great nerve, he had won an amazing 2,748 races from 8,084 rides, but found maintaining his racing weight increasingly difficult.

Melancholy from an early age, regular purging and fasting and the loss of his wife in childbirth are thought to have contributed to his death.

The painting of Fred Archer shows his traditional seat, rather slouched and with long stirrup leathers to accommodate his unusual length of leg – he stood 5ft 10ins tall. Shortly after his death a new style of riding was popularised in England by the American Tod Sloan – the so-called 'monkey up a stick' position. This was much faster, due to an improved centre of gravity and less wind resistance. This and his judgement of pace meant that Sloan was frequently on his own out in front – on his 'Tod'.

Steve Donoghue (1884 - 1945) won 14 British Classics and was Champion Jockey 10 years running from 1914 - 1923, sharing the last title with Charlie Elliott. Above all, Donoghue was a wonderful horseman who seemed to get the best out of all the horses he rode, rarely needing to use the whip. Donoghue was associated with two immortal horses – *The Tetrarch*, possibly the fastest racehorse on the British racecourse of the 20th century, and *Brown Jack*, his favourite.

Brown Jack
Bronze by Sir Alfred Munnings
Loan: The Sir Alfred Munnings Museum

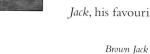

The most successful jockey in the history of British racing is Sir Gordon Richards, (1904 - 1986), with a career total of 4,870 winners. His record of 269 winners in a single year, 1947, also still stands. Strangely, it took him 28 attempts to win the Derby, an ambition which was finally realised on *Pinza* in 1953. Richards also holds the world record for riding the winners of successive races, because in 1933 he won the last race at Nottingham, all six at Chepstow the next day, and the first five, also at Chepstow, on the following day.

Front left to right   R. Perryman, R. Jones, C. Elliot, R. James, G. Richards, J. Collins,
S. Donoghue, W. Harding, W. Ramsden, J. Beasley, B. Lynch.
Rear left to right   A. Orme, M. J. Ellis, J. Leach, W. Lister, G. Hulme, S. Ingham, G. Smith, J. Patman,
W. H. McLachlan Jnr., C. Smirke, T. Weston, W. Howard, W. Alford, E. Gardner, W. Lammins.

*Manchester 1923 - Gordon Richards is front row fifth from the left, Steve Donoghue is seventh
from left, with his legs crossed*
Gift: Injured Jockeys Fund

Lester Piggott (Trevor Jones)

Lester Piggott (born 1935) ranks as a supremely gifted sportsman and the best-known jockey of his generation. During a career which spanned over forty years, he won the Derby an amazing nine times as well as a further twenty English Classics. With 4,493 wins to his credit, he is second only to Sir Gordon Richards in the league of most winning jockeys in Great Britain.

Popularly known as 'The Long Fellow', Lester Piggott rode incredibly short, yet still managed to balance his mounts with outstanding success. Despite a number of indiscretions he remained popular with the public who appreciated his competitive spirit. Lester was always famous for his economy with both words and money, but it was still a shock when he was sentenced to three years in prison in October 1987 for tax evasion. However, this has served to place him yet more firmly in the annals of racing history.

*Cigar box, whip and dressing case
belonging to Sir Gordon Richards*

*Saddle, earband and bronze of
Lester Piggott*

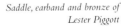

WILLIE CARSON'S INJURIES 1968 - 1996

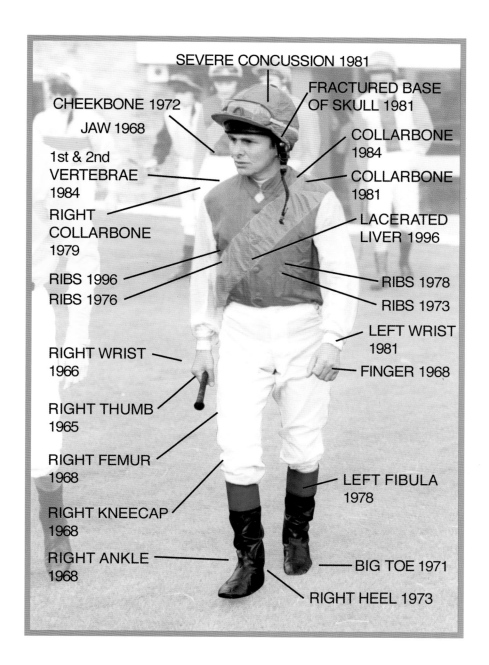

SEVERE CONCUSSION 1981

FRACTURED BASE OF SKULL 1981

CHEEKBONE 1972

JAW 1968

COLLARBONE 1984

1st & 2nd VERTEBRAE 1984

COLLARBONE 1981

RIGHT COLLARBONE 1979

LACERATED LIVER 1996

RIBS 1996

RIBS 1976

RIBS 1978

RIBS 1973

LEFT WRIST 1981

RIGHT WRIST 1966

FINGER 1968

RIGHT THUMB 1965

RIGHT FEMUR 1968

LEFT FIBULA 1978

RIGHT KNEECAP 1968

RIGHT ANKLE 1968

BIG TOE 1971

RIGHT HEEL 1973

Willie Carson OBE (born 1942) admits that he was not a natural jockey and needed to work extremely hard to learn the business. He almost gave up when his first three years of apprenticeship brought him no wins. However, by the end of his apprenticeship in 1965 he had ridden 58 winners, and when he retired he had 16 Classic wins to his credit.

In contrast, Pat Eddery is an instinctive rider. Although he was Champion Jockey at the age of 22 he spent much of his career in the shadow of Piggott's fame. Despite being based in Ireland for

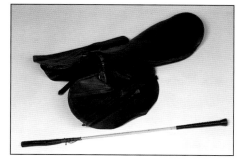

Exercise saddle and whip used by Willie Carson
Gift: Mr W. Carson

several years as retained jockey to Vincent O'Brien he has now amassed 11 championships here, the most recent in 1996. Now firmly part of the international racing scene, in 1997 Eddery won his 4000th race on *Silver Patriarch* in the St. Leger, making him - for now at least - behind only Richards and Piggott in terms of winners on the British turf.

The charismatic Frankie Dettori (born 1970) has caught the public's imagination, not least because of his feat of riding all seven winners on the first day of the prestigious Festival of Racing at Ascot in 1996. This result cost bookmakers millions and put several smaller ones out of business, but the overall effect was to bring attention back to racing at a time when it seemed almost overshadowed as a betting medium by the National Lottery.

Born in Italy, the son of Champion Italian jockey Gianfranco Dettori, Frankie came to Britain to serve his apprenticeship with Luca Cumani. Since then just about all the major races have come his way, and his famous leap from the saddle after a big race win has become his trademark. We are fortunate that he did not pursue his childhood ambition of being a petrol-pump attendant.

Many jockeys come from racing dynasties. Recent examples on the flat include Lester Piggott, Pat Eddery and Walter Swinburn and from an earlier generation it was true of Archer and many others. The current reigning champion (1998) is Keiren Fallon who reached the top in 1997 when he took over as retained jockey to Henry Cecil, having ridden with considerable success at a lower level for some years in the North.

Frankie Dettori
(Trevor Jones)

Frankie Dettori and the Colours worn by him on his magnificent seven winners at Ascot on 28 September 1996
Donated by the owners (Godolphin Management Company Ltd, Herbert Allen, J.C. Smith and Seisuke Hata) and by Frankie Dettori

The modern jockey can earn a great deal if successful. A few are paid a retainer so that a trainer or owner has first call on their services, and more receive a 'breeding right' for a winner which becomes a stallion, whereby they have the right to send a mare or sell the nomination annually. There is a fixed riding fee (currently £61.50 flat, £84.80 NH) plus a share of any prize money. Against this, however, jockeys have to meet considerable expenses from their earnings. A professional jockey may clock up 60,000 miles a year by car, helicopter and aeroplane in Britain alone. Added to this their career may not be very long, and they continually face the danger of injury or suspension. It is certainly true that racing is a dangerous and challenging profession to enter. Although the incidence of accidents may be lower than in sports such as rugby, soccer, cricket and athletics, when accidents do occur they are often very serious, despite ever-increasing Jockey Club regulations concerning head and body protection. Jockeys must also be extremely fit and strong - as a turn on the Museum's horse-simulator will show you. And of course, many have to pay almost constant attention to their weight, sweating in saunas and controlling their calorie intake minutely.

A day in the life of Jason Weaver (1994)

Up at 6.30am. Take half a cup of coffee with sugar and skimmed milk before having a quick look at *The Sporting Life* and *Racing Post*. Three mile run, takes me about a quarter of an hour.

Back home. More coffee and one slice of toast with Marmite. Bath and change. (I keep three bags permanently packed with my valets for the north, south and abroad so I do not need to think about what I need for the day.) Phone rings, agent and trainers. My agent updates rides for the day. Trainers who are not visiting the tracks phone through their orders. Driver collects me and we head off to Lingfield early for four rides;

Green Bio, trained by D. Chapman – came 4th

Bon Street, trained by J. Naughton – came 2nd

Silent Expression, trained by B. Meehan – came 1st (my 199th winner of the season!)
Stevie's Wonder, trained by T. Mills – came 3rd

Straight to the car and a two and a half to three hour drive to Wolverhampton for the evening meeting where I have three rides. No ride in the first, so I pick at a salad in the Weighing Room.

8.00pm race *Magna Carta*, trained by M. Stoute – came 1st (my ticket to the 200 Club!)

Rocketeer, trained by W. Muir – came 3rd

Allmosa, trained by J. Naughton – came 5th

Shower and change. Back in the car to be driven back to Newmarket by about 11pm, with a couple of glasses of bubbly to celebrate a busy but successful day.

In many ways this was a typical day for Jason Weaver, and many other jockeys who have to travel long distances between courses to ride for several different trainers on horses they may not meet until the race itself. Jason's was far from typical in one respect – his win on *Magna Carta* at Wolverhampton was his 200th win in a single season – a feat equalled by only a handful of jockeys. Jason Weaver trained at

MEDICAL CHECK

Every jockey has a Medical Record Book from the Jockey Club, in which injuries are recorded. It must be shown to the Medical Officers at the race meeting before the jockey weighs out. A bad fall can lead to a bar from riding for a period specified by the Medical Officer, and this is shown on the card.

The Jockey Club's Chief Medical Adviser is sent a report every raceday which lists injuries and falls, even outside the race itself. Although the injury rate is low compared to other sports, the nature of the injury tends to be serious. Apart from fractures, it is concussion which causes the most concern. On the Flat in Britain the concussion rate is about the same as for soccer, but the rate for amateur jump racing is nearly 35 times worse than soccer, with an injury rate which is four times smaller. Of the eight deaths in racing between 1974 and 1995 six were caused by massive head injuries. In terms of fatalities, the statistics show that Flat racing is twice as dangerous as motor racing, and four to five times more dangerous than driving on the roads. Taking into consideration jumping and point-to-point as well, racing has the highest rate of fatalities in any of the sports quoted in a recent 8-year study.

ADULT INJURY RATES

(Sheffield study, injuries per 1,000 participant days; racing per 1,000 rides)

Rugby	95.7
Soccer	64.4
Hockey	62.6
Mountaineering	56.2
Sailing	51.7
Cricket	48.7
Boxing/Martial arts	45.9
Motor Sports	29.7
Badminton	28.7
POINT-TO-POINT	**24.8**
Squash	23.9
Athletics	23.9
Tennis	23.1
JUMP, AMATEUR	**20.4**
Riding	16.1
Jump, Pro	10.4
Table Tennis	7.9
Swimming/diving	6.1
Golf	4.8
FLAT RACING	**1.4**

ADULT INJURY RATES

(8-year study, 799 deaths excluding natural causes; per 100m participant days; per 100m rides, over 21 year period)

POINT-TO-POINT	**811**
Climbing	793
Air sports	640+
JUMP RACING	**637**
FLAT RACING	**280**
Motor sport	145.8
Water sport	67.5
Sailing	44.5
Fishing (inc deep sea)	37.4
Riding (excl polo & hunting)	34.3
Soccer (over age 45)	26.0
Rugby	15.7
Skiing (estimated)	12.0
Boxing/wrestling	5.2
Gymnastics	4.8
Skating	4.7
Soccer	3.8
Cricket	3.1
Squash	0.9
Tennis	0.7

Lanfranco ridden by Frankie Dettori
at the Newmarket gallops
(Trevor Jones)

The Windsor Grand Military Steeplechase, 1840
by Francis Calcroft Turner
Gift: The Friends of the National Horseracing Museum

NATIONAL HUNT RACING

As its name suggests, National Hunt racing (which comprises steeplechasing, National Hunt flat races and hurdle races) developed from hunting. In the 1740s and 1750s foxhounds were crossed with greyhounds to provide a faster, lighter dog, and hunting too became faster. It very soon developed on occasion into a cross-country race with hounds, and then without hounds, from a given starting point towards some distant but visible target, often a church steeple. Steeplechases consisting of fences on a racecourse had taken place occasionally, beginning at Bedford in 1810, but modern steeplechasing is generally agreed to have been started at St. Albans by Thomas Coleman around 1830. It soon became popular and was emulated elsewhere, such as at Cheltenham in 1834, the Vale of Aylesbury in 1835, and at Aintree in 1836.

The first Aintree steeplechases attracted few runners and were heavily criticised for cruelty to the horses. The first true Grand National is generally accepted to be that of 1839, and was won by the appropriately named *Lottery*, whose party tricks included jumping over dining tables. Thanks to the new railways and improved roads, an estimated fifty thousand people crowded the course. They saw the famous Captain Becher fall into the brook which thereafter bore his name, but probably missed his complaint that 'water is no damned use without brandy'.

Lottery's rider, Jem Mason, was a professional in a sport dominated in its early days by wealthy amateurs who frequently had a military connection. Another famous professional of the period was Tom Olliver, who won four Grand Nationals. Towards the end of the century amateurs such as Arthur Yates, George Ede and Maunsell Richardson competed on equal terms with the professionals, but subsequently the sport became very largely professional. Later the Brown brothers carried the flag for the amateurs between the wars and Harry was the last amateur to head the jockeys' list in 1919.

The early Grand Nationals were somewhat robust, emulating the cavalry's dare-devil skill and courage in the saddle. In several of the early years the field had to jump a solid stone wall. Public outcry against cruelty to horse and rider was immediate. Over the years, the course, prize money, training and administration were all thankfully improved.

The early days of steeplechasing were marred by a lack of rules and too many small meetings which attracted defaulters and touts.

Sergeant Murphy jumping Becher's Brook
by Lionel Edwards, 1923
Gift: The Macdonald–Buchanan Family Charitable Trust

The Jockey Club, in the person of Admiral Rous, was distinctly sniffy about National Hunt racing, and considered it an 'extraneous branch' of the sport. Nevertheless, in 1866 six members of the Club joined seven others to form the National Hunt Committee, which attempted to set regulations and, rather less successfully, to enforce them. This Committee was not absorbed into the Jockey Club until 1969 although throughout its life it had a fair proportion of members in common.

Autobiography of Arthur Yates,
Trainer and Gentleman rider
Gift: Mrs A. Bridgeman

Before the advent of the National Hunt Committee jumping lost its early popularity as fences got ridiculously small and 'cocktail' horses were entered. However, although steeplechasing in general came in for much criticism, the Grand National was extremely well attended and provided the best test of a good jumper. Patronage by the Prince of Wales, still the only Royal owner to have won the Grand National (with *Ambush II* in 1900) did much to promote National Hunt racing, but it remained very much the poor relation of the Flat. As a result, there were few dominant owners.

This changed a little in the interwar years, when wealthy Americans such as J. H. Whitney and Mr & Mrs F. Ambrose Clark became involved. With them came a speeding up of the races and a corresponding change in the style of riding.

Likewise, in the early days National Hunt trainers did not really exist as a separate and identifiable group. Horses were part of their owners' hunting lives and were often under the same charge. Even with the Grand National very few trainers of winners are identifiable prior to the 1880s. A major early trainer at the turn of the century was Arthur Yates (1841 – 1922), who was a successful amateur rider before training very successfully at Alresford, Hampshire. Amongst other winners, he trained *Roquefort* (Grand National 1885) and *Cloister* (Grand National 1893). The latter's Grand National win was in a then record time (9 min 32 2/5 sec) with a record weight (12.7 stones) and by a record distance (40 lengths). The status of training in Victorian England was made clear enough by the fact that both were offically trained by one of his head lads, Swatton.

Cloister by Joshua Dighton (op 1860-1899)
Purchase

In contrast, Tom Coulthwaite (1862 – 1948) claimed never to have sat on a horse, but learned his trade by training Victorian athletes. He trained three National winners, *Eremon, Jenkinstown* and *Grakle*, during a long career and despite being warned off from 1913 to 1930 over the running of a horse called *Bloodstone*.

The Cheltenham Gold Cup was founded in 1924 to provide a conditions race where all horses would meet on an equal basis, with an age

allowance for five-year-olds and now also with one for
mares of 5lb. This was to contrast with the Grand
National, where handicapping meant that all the
horses' chances were equal, at least in theory. By the
thirties the race was established in its own right rather
than as a preliminary to the National, and has rarely
been won by a moderate horse. The Champion
Hurdle, performing the same function over the smaller
obstacles, quickly followed in 1927.

*Models of 'Golden Miller', 'Desert Orchid' and 'Arkle'
with the Cheltenham Gold Cup from 1939
won by 'Brendan's Cottage'*

From 1932 to 1938 the Gold Cup was dominated
by *Golden Miller*, who won it five times. Like many
legendary horses, *Golden Miller* was unimpressive at
first, and was bought and sold several times. However as a four-year-old his jumping ability was enough to
persuade the impressively eccentric Dorothy Paget to buy him for £6,000.

Dorothy Paget financed her horseracing interests with a vast inherited fortune. She made up for plainness of
appearance by having almost too much character. Her trainers, which she changed regularly, had to put up with
night-time phone calls, because she dined at 7am, slept through the day and had breakfast at 8.30pm followed by
vast meals throughout the night. She disliked humans, especially men, who were said to make her vomit. When

The winner Golden Miller leading the field in the 1934 Grand National by Martin Stainforth. **Purchase**

she kissed *Golden Miller* after one of his many victories, an observer speculated that this was probably the first time she had kissed a member of the opposite sex - and a gelding, at that.

Golden Miller's first Cheltenham Gold Cup was a somewhat hollow victory, the better horses falling like ninepins at the very severe fences. The following year he was the favourite and won by ten lengths, but made a mistake, lost his confidence and later fell in the Grand National. However, in 1934 he became the only horse ever to win both the Cheltenham Gold Cup and the Grand National in the same year.

Peter Cazalet (1907-1973) was always high in the list of leading trainers between 1958 and 1970, despite bad luck with both the Grand National and the Cheltenham Gold Cup. His worst blow was when *Devon Loch* (ridden by Dick Francis) spread-eagled within 50 yards of the winning post; but he trained over 250 winners for the Queen Mother. After his death, the Queen Mother transferred her horses to Fulke Walwyn, another great name in post-war National Hunt training, who had ridden *Reynoldstown* to one of his National wins in 1936.

The third major trainer of this period was Ryan Price, most of whose many winners were ridden by Fred Winter and Josh Gifford. The latter took over his jumpers in 1970 when he decided to concentrate on the flat.

Fred Winter and Fred Rimell share the distinction of having been both Champion Jockey and Leading Trainer. Winter (b. 1926) retired from his remarkable riding career in 1964. Perhaps his finest hour came in 1962 when the bit broke in the horse's mouth on the gallant *Mandarin* before halfway in the Grand Steeplechase de Paris and yet, miraculously, the pair still won despite the horse himself breaking down in what was to prove his final race. Those who saw it still swear it was the most remarkable sight ever seen on a racecourse. He quickly succeeded in

his new career and won the Grand National in 1965 with *Jay Trump* followed by a win with *Anglo* in 1966. His successes made him Leading Trainer seven times. Rimell had 34 winners as a flat jockey, before turning to National Hunt in 1932. He was Champion Jockey four times before injury finished his riding career, and then Leading Trainer four times.

Training from Co Tipperary, Vincent O'Brien won the Cheltenham Gold Cup three times in a row from 1948 with *Cottage Rake*, and the Grand National with *Early Mist* in 1953, *Royal Tan* in 1954 and *Quare Times* in 1955, as well as many other important National Hunt races. In 1959 he abandoned jumping and devoted himself to the flat, with outstanding and consistent results.

Champion National Hunt horses are almost invariably geldings (for obvious reasons) and so are not taken out of racing to go to stud. There is therefore an opportunity for horses like *Golden Miller* to win the Grand National or Cheltenham Gold Cup more than once, and thus to establish their personalities and become legends. Only one horse has won the Grand National three times - the immortal *Red Rum*, who also came second twice.

Only *Manifesto* can get near this record - winner in 1897 and 1899 and third three times, once carrying 12st 13lbs, whilst six others have won twice. *Cottage Rake* and *Arkle* each won three Cheltenham Gold Cups. *Cottage Rake*, trained by a young Vincent O'Brien and ridden by Aubrey Brabazon, was greeted by the following ditty at Cheltenham:

"Aubrey's up, the money's down
The frightened bookies quake
Come on my lads and give a cheer
Begod, 'tis Cottage Rake."

Arkle and Mill House in the 1965 Cheltenham Gold Cup
by Lionel Edwards
Purchase

Arkle inspired an even more enthusiastic following. Foaled in 1957, he was bought by Anne, Duchess of Westminster, and named after a mountain on her estate in Sutherland. His first Cheltenham Gold Cup, in 1964, was a duel with *Mill House,* his exact contemporary and long-time rival. During the next three years only four horses finished ahead of him, and by the time he retired due to injury in 1966 he had won a total of 27 races. He was trained by Tom Dreaper (1898 – 1975) who was also responsible for four other great Irish horses, *Prince Regent, Royal Approach, Flyingbolt,* and *Fortria.*

Red Rum

Loan: Mr & Mrs D. McCain

It seemed unlikely that another horse would capture the public imagination in the same way, but *Red Rum's* three Grand National wins (1973, 1974, 1977) coupled with his showbusiness personality brought National Hunt racing to new levels of popularity.

Aldaniti's 1981 Grand National win was also the stuff of legends. Foaled in 1970, the chestnut had a poor pedigree and suffered recurring lameness. In 1979, his jockey Bob Champion was told that he had cancer, and had only eight months to live. The story of the pair's recovery and subsequent victory was told in the film 'Champions'.

Desert Orchid, known to millions as '*Dessie*', captured the public imagination, due to his grey colour, his character and his remarkable ability. Again, his success came in spite of a mixed pedigree and early disasters, and although highly successful in other major races over hurdles and then fences, it took him until 1989 to win the Cheltenham Gold Cup. He retired in 1991 aged 12, and, like *Red Rum,* has become a celebrity thanks to numerous public appearances.

The most recent horse to become a legend is *One Man,* tragically killed at Aintree in April 1998. His 20 wins included both the King George VI (1995 and 1996), Hennessy Gold Cup and the Queen Mother Champion Chase at Cheltenham less than a month before his death, and again his personality and temperament made him popular with the public. His northern-based trainer, Gordon Richards (b. 1930), died the same year.

Peter Scudamore MBE (b. 1958) started his career as an amateur, combining it with work as an estate agent, before turning professional after riding his first

Desert Orchid winner of the
Cheltenham Gold Cup by J. Adamson

Gift: J. Adamson

*Racing boots, breeches and body
protector worn by Peter Scudamore*
Gift: Peter Scudamore

winner in 1979. He made history in the 1988-89 season when he clocked up 221 winners, but success in the Grand National (which his father had won on *Oxo* in 1959) eluded him. By the time of his retirement in 1993 he had a winning tally of 1678 races, and had been National Hunt Champion Jockey seven times, sharing the title once with his great adversary and friend, John Francome, Fred Winter's main jockey and also a multiple champion.

Richard Dunwoody (b. 1964) is still closely associated in the public mind with *Desert Orchid*, on whom he won seven races. He has also won the Grand National twice to date. He has now overtaken Peter Scudamore's record of National Hunt wins.

The rise of the present champion Tony McCoy has been meteoric. He was sports mad from an early age and sat on a horse almost before he could walk. He joined Tony Balding's Hampshire Stables in 1994 at the age of 19, and by the end of the 94/95 season was champion conditional jockey. The next two seasons each saw him as champion jockey. He won the 1997 Cheltenham Gold Cup on *Mr Mulligan*, despite having broken both shoulder bones two months before.

Jenny Pitman with Burrough Hill Lad, winner of the Cheltenham Gold Cup, Welsh Grand National, and Hennessy Cognac Gold Cup. Pitman is the only woman trainer to have won the Grand National, with Corbiere in 1983 and Royal Athlete in 1995 (Gerry Cranham)

SPECTATORS AND PLUNGERS

Although it is not essential to bet in order to enjoy an afternoon at the races, betting has been an important part of racing history since Roman times. It became even more serious in the 18th century, when gentlemen owners laid odds against each other's horses in addition to the sums put up as matches. Bets were laid in clubs and drawing rooms, and indeed the Museum is housed in the old Subscription Rooms where men came to settle their bets.

These gentlemen bet not only on the races but also on cards, cock-fights, coursing, bare-knuckle fighting, running footmen, and in fact just about anything. One man won a bet that he could find someone to eat a live cat. Others raced against the clock or over incredible distances.

On the racecourse, bets were made at the betting post - the remains of Newmarket's is now in the Museum. It was not until about 1800 that the concept of making a book came into vogue - i.e. offering various odds on all the runners in a race. Thus the bookmaker was born. Betting was encouraged still further by the introduction of handicapping, and spectators' enjoyment by the resultant increased fields and by improved facilities at the racecourses. In 1839 spectators were prevented from riding just behind the runners, as they had for two centuries at Newmarket. Many courses had no barriers, and indeed the early concept of a rail was to stop people interfering with the race rather than to protect them from possible injury.

Subscription Rooms at Newmarket, 1825 print after James Pollard　　　　　　　　　　　　**Gift: Mrs R. Legouix**

A medley of bookmakers and bettors, known as the Ring, would follow the races, overwhelming each town in turn. Many 'legs' or bookmakers had dubious backgrounds and worse morals. Since thousands of guineas could rest on the outcome of a race, crime abounded. Touts hid behind bushes on the Heath to spy on gallops, matches were fixed, horses pulled, and ringers run. Serious doubts exist about several Derby winners, including *Bloomsbury* and one or two of Lord Egremont's five winners, which may well have been four rather than three years old. *Running Rein*, winner of the 1844 Derby, was afterwards proved to be the four-year-old *Maccabeus*.

Nobbling, too, was frequent. Between 1809 and 1811, four racehorses died and others were very sick after drinking poisoned water from a trough on Newmarket Heath. Following the offer of a £500 reward for information leading to an arrest, suspicion fell upon Daniel Dawson, a tout in the pay of two bookmakers.

Dawson's accomplice, a disreputable chemist called Cecil Bishop, turned King's Evidence and Dawson stood trial at Cambridge Assizes in July 1812. He was convicted, sentenced to death and hanged in front of 15,000 people. The two bookmakers at the bottom of the scandal escaped unscathed.

Many bookmakers did very well from their profession. John Gully (1783-1863), retired champion prize-fighter, branched out into ownership but was hoist by his own petard when his horse *Mameluke* lost the 1827 St. Leger. He

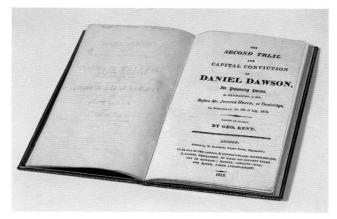

The Second Trial and Capital Conviction of Daniel Dawson

had backed it to win £40,000, but bribery had been used to unsettle the favourite through a series of false starts. The blackguard involved, William Crockford, made enough money from the affair to set up a gaming house. He in his turn suffered. In 1844 his *Ratan* was probably got at and certainly pulled; he died on the morning of the Oaks shortly afterwards but legend says was propped up in the window of his gaming club so that his losing bets on the Derby could still be collected.

Meanwhile Gully consolidated his fortune, owned other winners of the Derby and St. Leger, and allied himself

with Harry Hill, another bookmaker who was said to have several jockeys in his pocket. Gully further increased his wealth from coalmining and became an MP. Hill lost all his money on the Stock Exchange.

Others made money from gambling. Dennis O'Kelly (d. 1787) arrived penniless from Ireland and spent time in a debtors' prison, but became a highly successful gambler, owner and breeder. After successfully predicting '*Eclipse* first and the rest nowhere' for the second heat of *Eclipse's* first outing, he bought a half-share in the horse for 750 guineas and added the other half later for 1,100 guineas. He was estimated to have made at least £25,000 from him at stud alone.

However, many lost fortunes through gambling. The life of the Marquis of Hastings (1842-1868) was used as an awful warning; rich and self-indulgent, even at Eton he fell prey to vultures. Even though he won £70,000 when his horse *Lecturer* won the Cesarewitch in 1866, it could have been far more if he had not been too drunk to remember some of his large bets. Hastings eloped with Mr Henry Chaplin's fiancée just before the wedding, but in 1867 Hastings lost £120,000 when Chaplin's *Hermit* won the Derby. His wife, Lady Florence Paget, chose badly as Chaplin became a cabinet minister and Viscount whereas Hastings fell into the clutches of an evil money-lender named Padwick. He was forced to scratch one of his 1868 Derby hopes the evening before the race but the scratched horse, *The Earl*, promptly won the Grand Prix in Paris and three races at Royal Ascot within a five day period. *Lady Elizabeth*, his remaining Derby hope, had lost her form and with it his last hope of financial salvation. He died penniless a few months later.

As we have seen, Lord George Bentinck - who was the heaviest bettor in Britain - did much to reform the Turf, both in reducing fraud and improving facilities for spectators. Officially, the Jockey Club washed its hands of betting disputes in 1843, and it remains true that wagers are not recoverable in law.

There were other ways of losing money. Frith's famous Derby Day shows pickpockets, card sharps, find the lady operators, lucky heather sellers and tipsters, all of whom exist today, if in a more restricted way. Derby Day at this period was so popular that even the House of Commons adjourned for it, and people of all classes came to Epsom, as they still do. The affluent viewed from private boxes or their carriages parked along the course, while most of the rest watched from the Downs.

Prince Monolulu's jackets
Gift: The Friends of the National Horseracing Museum

Card-sellers emerged as a breed in about 1835, walking the miles between racecourses, and, later, travelling by rail mostly without tickets. Tipsters are first recorded in the 1840s; by the 1850s the newspapers were full of their adverts. Many were characters in their own right so that perhaps nobody minded too much if the tips didn't work out. Later, Prince Ras Monolulu's (d. 1965) cheerful cry of '*I gotta horse*', carried him before Royalty and made him a national figure. His account of his early life as a stowaway was as fanciful as his fortune-telling, his outfits and his pretensions to royalty.

There have been a number of legislative attempts to control betting. The spectacular mid-Victorian boom, particularly in pubs, led to the banning of off-course cash betting in 1853; cash transactions went under the counter, while the upper classes still bet on credit, which was perfectly legal. Bookies were allowed on the course, however, and at every meeting the different areas - though not the Members' Enclosure - would be crammed with their stands, the major operators in the centre, the small-timers hovering on the edge where quick escape was possible.

Until 1961, off-course cash betting remained illegal. However betting took place in pubs, factories and workshops, with children often acting as 'bookies' runners' to collect the stakes.

The Betting, Gaming and Lotteries Act of 1961 reflected the Government's belated realisation that betting should be regulated and legalised. No doubt they realised that it could then be taxed, which, soon enough, it was. However, High Street betting shops had to be very unattractive, without televisions or other inducements to enjoyment. Results were transmitted via the Exchange Telegraph Company. There were soon 15,000 such shops.

In 1963 Ladbrokes had started a new trend by opening a book on the contest for the Tory leadership, and the following year £600,000 was bet with them on the General Election, including probably the world's biggest bet at that time, of £50,000. The way was open for betting on all sorts of things – Eurovision song contests, cricket, snow at Christmas, and much more. The first major revision of the Act took place in 1986. At last some degree of comfort was permitted. Television sets arrived and the SIS cable service was established.

There is a constant tension between the bookmaking industry and Racing as to the level of betting levy which should be returned to the sport. As well as this percentage, Racing benefits from the profits of the Tote. This was set up by Parliament in 1928 as the Racecourse Betting Control Board (now the Horserace Totalisator Board) as a publicly-run pool betting system. The Tote remains the only body allowed to carry out pool betting, whereby all the money bet on a race forms a pool from which the dividend is paid after the race. Unlike betting with a bookmaker, the punter does not know how much he or she will win until the dividend is calculated.

The word 'Tote' originates from the adding machines which were originally used to count and register the tickets sold. The Tote was computerised in the 1980s, so that dividends can be declared within seconds of the official result being announced.

Racing is still a national passion today. About five million people a year attend the races, many more watch it on television, and racing is the only sport with a dedicated daily newspaper. Racing is truly a national sport – it appeals to all ages, all social classes and a much higher proportion of women – attracting a more representative sample of the British population than probably any other spectator sport.

In 1997 a sociologist, Kate Fox, studied racegoers and their habits. She wanted to know why racing crowds do not behave like people in other public settings: 'at the races, complete strangers not only make frequent eye contact, but also smile at each other for no apparent reason, and even initiate conversation'. She concluded, amongst other things, that social behaviour at the races is governed by a relaxation of normal restrictions and restraints combined with an exaggeration of social rules and controls almost to the point of caricature. This allows racegoers to adopt any role or social status they choose. Above all, 'racegoers are united in the common purpose of enjoyment'.

Contemporary copy of Derby Day
by William Powell Frith
Anonymous Loan

SELECT BIBLIOGRAPHY

A Race Apart; The History of the Grand National,
Reg Green, Hodder & Stoughton London

1988 Encyclopaedia of Steeplechasing
Compiled by Patricia Smyly, Robert Hale London 1979

The Channel Four Book of Racing;
Sean Magee, Hamlyn London Revised

1995 Biographical Encyclopaedia of British Flat Racing;
Roger Mortimer/ Richard Onslow/Peter Willett,
Macdonald & Jane's Ltd. London 1978

Bred for the Purple; Michael Seth-Smith,
Leslie Frewin Publishers Ltd. London 1969

Great Racing Gambles & Frauds Vols 1 & 2 Ed; Richard Onslow,
Marlborough Books Swindon 1991 & 1992

Racing Art and Memorabilia; Graham Budd,
Philip Wilson Publishers in association with
The National Horseracing Museum London 1997

Headquarters; Richard Onslow, Great Ouse Press Cambridge 1983

The History of Horse Racing;
Roger Longrigg, Macmillan London 1972

The Guinness Book of Great Jockeys of the Flat,
Michael Tanner & Gerry Cranham,
Guinness Publishing Enfield 1992

The Racing Tribe – the social behaviour of horsewatchers;
Kate Fox, Social Issues Research Centre London 1997

The Great Racehorses; Julian Wilson,
Little, Brown & Company Revised Edition, London 1998

Ferries *of* DOVER
THROUGH FIVE DECADES 1960–2011

John Hendy

Ferry Publications

Published by:
Ferry Publications, PO Box 33, Ramsey, Isle of Man IM99 4LP
Tel: +44 (0) 1624 898445   Fax: +44 (0) 1624 898449
E-mail: ferrypubs@manx.net   Website: www.ferrypubs.co.uk

Introduction

Living and being educated in Dover during the immediate post-war period, some of my earliest memories were of seeing cars being crane loaded at the Admiralty Pier aboard the British Railways car ferry *Dinard*. Another daily feature was the 'Golden Arrow' steamer *Invicta* while berths 3 and 4 would invariably contain sleek and powerful units of the Belgian Marine fleet, perhaps the *Koning Albert* or the *Prince Baudouin*. At the lay-by berth, out at number 5, was frequently the *Isle of Thanet*, awaiting her summer season on the Folkestone – Boulogne service while in the Granville and Wellington Docks there was always the chance of seeing one of the local BR units undergoing refit from the adjacent Packet Yard – this in itself a name steeped in history.

On the Admiralty Pier, puffs of smoke and white steam indicated the presence of steam locomotives from diminutive shunters busying themselves with parcel wagons to the gleaming green Bullied 'Pacific' class engines which hauled the Boat Trains from London's Victoria station to the line's end under Dover Marine's blackened roof. Nearby a twin-funnelled train ferry sat partly hidden in the specially constructed Ferry Dock which allowed the rails on board the ship to align with the rails ashore.

It was a scene of noise, tremendous activity and of constant ship movements as the sea-links between Ostend, Dunkirk, Calais and Boulogne were maintained with clockwork regularity. What is more, all the ships (apart from Townsend's single vessel) were painted with black hulls, white upperworks and with buff, black topped funnels. Any thought of using them for advertising was preposterous!

Who then could have believed that this idyllic situation would and could ever change?

During the past 50 years I have witnessed a complete transport revolution. Whereas Dover (and other traditional ferry ports) relied on efficient rail connections and stations adjacent to the quaysides, the opening of the Eastern Docks car ferry terminal in 1953 catered for an entirely different type of traveller. Being tourist generated, this traffic remained mainly seasonal in nature and there was restricted work for the handful of car ferries out of season until 1965 when the carriage of lorry traffic suddenly revolutionised the vehicle ferry trade and required a total reinvention of basic cross-Channel ferry design.

Whereas the Government-controlled fleets of Britain, France and Belgium were slow to react to the changes and were always reluctant to invest in new tonnage due to the possibility of a Channel Tunnel being built, Townsend Bros. Car Ferries, who until this time had been a minority player in the cross-Channel scene, was quick to see the opportunities and within 12 years had introduced eight 'Free Enterprise' class ships and also established Zeebrugge as a major ferry port. Eventually when the nationalised companies did respond, it was a case of too little too late.

At the Admiralty Pier, the long-established passenger-only vessels were gradually withdrawn and replaced by vehicle carrying ships. A linkspan was built at berth 4 in 1974 and now Ostend sailings carried both rail-connected passengers in addition to cars and freight but as the Eastern Docks expanded, so traffic ebbed away from the traditional exit point. The final passenger only steamer was the former Channel Islands ship, *Caesarea* which finished service in 1980. The following year briefly came the much-travelled *Caledonian Princess* before the retired car/ train ferry *Chartres* finally closed the traditional Dover – Calais rail-connected service in September 1993.

By then, the British Government had de-nationalised its shipping division, Sealink, and the Ostend service operated by the Belgians had moved to Ramsgate with a final and totally unsuccessful attempt to make the route pay. Townsend (the European Ferries Group) was taken over by P&O late in 1986 while Sealink – owned following de-nationalisation by Sea Containers of Bermuda – was eventually swallowed up by the Swedish operators, Stena Line.

With the final opening of the long-awaited Channel Tunnel in 1994, Stena and P&O embarked on a joint-venture in 1998 with the latter company taking a 60%-40% share before Stena withdrew four years later. This left P&O Ferries in competition with SeaFrance, the only surviving nationalised ferry company, although the start of a new Danish-backed service to Dunkirk in 2000 has proved to be a success. Initially starting with new ro-pax ships, Norfolkline introduced three larger ships during 2005/06. The Maersk subsidiary company was taken over by fellow Danish company, DFDS Seaways in 2010.

The opening of the Channel Tunnel reduced the need to continue the Dunkirk train ferry service although it continued until 1995 when the remaining vessel was withdrawn and switched to carry freight on the Calais route.

During this latter period, two attempts have been made to restart the service from Dover to Boulogne but both have met in failure, this in spite of the French authorities building a new ferry port in the outer harbour at Boulogne. LD Lines, the French company who were the last to operate the link, had even attempted to operate an overnight sailing from Dover to Dieppe but the traffic just wasn't there.

'Ferries of Dover' aims to show the development and changes at the port during the last 50 years. This also includes the port of Folkestone which carried significant traffic, latterly to Boulogne only, until axed by Stena Line in 1991. Thereafter a service was continued using Hoverspeed's catamarans and also with a variety of marginal freight operators until the last of these folded in 2001.

What will the next decade bring? With the Eastern Docks now approaching capacity, Dover Harbour Board has given the green light for the construction of a new terminal at the Western Docks. Whereas the port's expansion will be a positive step for Dover, it is with great sadness that much of the historical heart of the port will be swept away in order to achieve this goal. Not only this but public access to the port and its ships will in future be severely restricted by the closure of the Prince of Wales' Pier – of long and happy memory.

John Hendy

The 1960s

The passing of the *Isle of Thanet* (in 1963) and the *Canterbury* (in 1964) severed the port's cross-Channel connections with the 1920s. These elegant ships represented an entirely different era of travel, the latter being forever associated with the glittering First Class 'Golden Arrow' service which had started in May 1929.

The decade saw the start of the roll on – roll off revolution when in September 1965, Townsend Car Ferries announced that they would "accept the immediate shipment of freight". Until that period, the car ferry industry was very much seasonal in nature with summer tourist traffic surging ahead while winter trade was minimal. The advent of lorry traffic created problems for ferry operators as existing vehicle deck headroom and stern-loading facilities were soon outmoded. As this aspect of the industry grew and prospered, Dover Eastern Docks expanded with new berths. Meanwhile traffic at the Admiralty Pier (Western Docks) remained passenger only/ train connected but the writing was now on the wall as the inevitable decline in traffic set in.

Townsend Bros. Car Ferries Ltd withdrew their converted frigate *Halladale* in 1961 and the following year saw the arrival of the *Free Enterprise* – shocking in her 'Caronia' green livery.

British Railways became British Rail in 1964 and a new logo and livery were introduced. The main thrust of their local car ferry service remained Boulogne and in 1969, their first diesel-powered vessel entered service. This was the versatile *Vortigern* which was intended for Dover-Boulogne car ferry work during the summer and the Dunkirk train ferry out of season.

In 1967 Townsend introduced their *Autocarrier*; a converted freight ship for the newly opened Zeebrugge service. In the previous year, Belgian Marine's *Prinses Paola* became the very last traditional passenger-only ferry to be built. The differing business strategies between the operators was enormous and Ostend suffered while Zeebrugge flourished.

Towards the end of her final season in service, the veteran passenger steamer *Isle of Thanet* (of 1925) was taken out of service after colliding with a jetty in Boulogne. With the *Lord Warden* switched to cover her sailings, she retired to the Granville Dock at Dover for repairs. Here she is on 6th August 1963, leaving Dover under her own steam for the final time.

Throughout the 50s and 60s, Dover's 'star turn' was the 'Golden Arrow' steamer *Invicta*. Spending 19 hours each day alongside at the Admiralty Pier, hers was a life of luxury which befitted British Railways' high status London - Paris through service via Dover - Calais.

The *Canterbury* inaugurated the 'Golden Arrow' service in May 1929 but after the post-war introduction of the *Invicta*, spent most of her later career on the seasonal Folkestone - Boulogne route. Finishing service the year after the *Isle of Thanet*, she is seen arriving at Dover for her final period of lay-up in September 1964.

The turbine steamer *Lord Warden* (1952) was England's first purpose-built car ferry, carrying 120 vehicles on the Dover - Boulogne route. Eventually replaced by more modern units, she finished her days at Holyhead before being sold to Saudi Arabian owners in 1979.

The elegant *Maid of Kent* joined the fleet in 1959 and is seen going astern onto the Admiralty Pier shortly after the application of her new BR livery early in 1965. In 1974 she was switched to the Weymouth - Cherbourg route and survived until 1981 by which time she had become her owners' last steam-powered cross-Channel ship.

Built as a passenger steamer for the overnight Southampton - Le Havre route, in 1963 the *Normannia* was sent to the Tyne to be converted into a car ferry for the Dover - Boulogne route. With capacity for just 550 passengers and 110 cars, the diminutive ferry was later used on the Channel Islands services.

The Dover - Dunkirk train ferry service commenced in October 1936 and was operated by three identical sister ships. Here is the *Shepperton Ferry* leaving Dover in September 1964 shortly before being repainted in British Rail colours and casting a characteristic smoke plume across the harbour.

The *Hampton Ferry* is seen coming astern towards the Train Ferry Dock, the black balls from her main mast indicating that she is using her bow rudder. She was replaced in the local fleet in 1969 by the *Vortigern* and operated as a freight vessel during the final few months of her career.

One of the joys of the off-season was the appearance of the railway steamers in Dover's inner docks for refit by the nearby Packet Yard. In this April 1968 view, the new car ferry *Dover* lies alongside the former Great Western Railway steamer *St. Patrick* which had joined the local fleet late in 1964.

The brand new *Vortigern* is seen entering Dover Harbour from Boulogne during her first week of service in August 1969. As the first diesel-powered ferry in the local railway fleet, the highly versatile vessel doubled as a Dunkirk train ferry during the winter months.

Although associated throughout her career with the Folkestone - Calais service, the French passenger steamer *Cote d'Azur* made occasional weekend visits to Dover during the summer season. She was withdrawn from service in September 1972.

During the winter of 1966-67, the new Channel Islands steamer *Caesarea* was brought up Channel to deputise on the 'Golden Arrow' service. Seen during early January 1967 (note the Christmas tree on her fore mast), the ship leaves the Western Entrance in style.

The *St. Patrick* is seen arriving at Dover from Calais in January 1967. Used mainly on the seasonal Folkestone - Boulogne route from 1965-71, she was also used to relieve on the Calais routes or to operate additional 'Agents' Specials'.

The first French (SNCF) car ferry was the *Compiegne* of 1958 which is seen leaving Dover Eastern Docks in June 1965. A very modern ship for her day, she was built with a stern docking bridge for Dover arrivals although in practice it was rarely used. The open door to her vehicle deck was a regular sight in those carefree days.

The *Compiegne* was joined by the *Chantilly* in 1966 and both worked the Calais route until joined by the ships of British Rail to combat the growing Townsend Car Ferries in 1970. The *Chantilly* was latterly used on the secondary Newhaven - Dieppe link.

The third of the pre-war Dunkirk train ferries was the *Twickenham Ferry* which was handed over to French control (hence ALA on her funnels) in 1936. She was beautifully maintained and was the last of the trio in service, not being withdrawn until May 1974.

The original *Free Enterprise* entered service between Dover and Calais in April 1962. A compact little vessel capable of carrying 120 cars and a vehicle deck high enough for lorries (should that traffic ever materialise), she continued in service until Christmas 1979 after which she was sold to Greek owners.

The *Free Enterprise II* is seen arriving at Dover on the occasion of her maiden commercial voyage from Calais in May 1965. The least successful of the Townsend fleet, she was always hampered by her low vehicle deck height which proved unsuitable for lorries.

The *Free Enterprise III* is seen moving off her berth on the morning of her arrival from her Dutch builders in July 1966. Townsend's ability to order new ships for the following season saw them mount the first serious challenge to the joint BR/SNCF nationalised ferry fleets.

The *Free Enterprise IV* leaving Dover in August 1969. The addition of a 4-hour service to Zeebrugge in 1966 had seen the company make huge inroads into the established Ostend route and the start of a freight revolution which demanded a complete rethink in ferry design.

When the General Steam Navigation Company's Eagle Steamers closed their excursion business in 1966, Townsend's parent company acquired the *Royal Sovereign* and converted her into a freight ship for the Dover - Zeebrugge route. Although not an unqualified success, she paved the way before being sold to Italian interests as the *Ischia* in October 1973.

The first purpose-built car ferry for the Ostend - Dover link was the elegant *Car Ferry* in 1949. Three years later she was renamed *Prinses Josephine Charlotte* and was crane loaded at the Admiralty Pier until the Eastern Docks terminal was opened in 1953. Her capacity was latterly for just for 90 cars.

Belgian Marine introduced their second car ferry in 1958. The *Artevelde* was unusual in not carrying a 'royal' name and is seen leaving Dover's berth 1 during 1966. With capacity for 160 cars, her narrow stern entrance made the carriage of freight difficult although her beautiful sleek lines typified the Ostend fleet of this era.

A third Ostend car ferry entered service in 1962. The *Koningin Fabiola* is seen entering Dover in August 1969 and displays similar lines to those of her half sister *Artevelde*. In order to cater for rail-connected passengers, in winter 1976-77 she had her upper vehicle deck converted into passenger spaces thereby reducing car capacity to just 88.

The *Roi Baudouin* of 1965 is seen coming astern at berth 1 during her maiden season in service. Her raked masts introduced a new look for the Belgian Marine fleet as all their previous diesel-powered vessels had been fitted with vertical masts.

A fifth Belgian car ferry was the *Princesse Astrid* on 1968. To all intents and purposes a copy of the *Roi Baudouin*, the black top to her funnel was deeper and they were therefore easy to tell apart. Graceful she may have been but the vehicle deck lay-out had not changed in ten years.

Taken in the summer of 1962, this image of the pioneer Belgian Marine diesel-powered ferry *Prince Baudouin* (1934) sees her during her penultimate season by which time her use was very spasmodic. Notice the twin salvage vessels at work in the Western Entrance which was not opened until April 1963.

Such was the success of the 'Baudouin' that she was followed by the *Prins Albert* in October 1937. She is seen arriving at Dover in September 1964 her characteristic open decks, squat funnel and vertical pole masts giving her a very powerful look. A third sister ship, *Prince Philippe*, was a war casualty and failed to enter commercial service.

The post-war passenger vessel *Koning Albert* (1947) was Belgian Marine's centenary vessel. She is unusually seen leaving Folkestone for Ostend in 1967 during a period when the Western Docks was being dredged. In favourable conditions, the Ostend passenger vessels could make the crossing in 3 hours.

The *Roi Leopold III* was the first of three sister ships built between 1956 and 1958 to coincide with the expected surge of traffic for the Brussels Universal Exhibition. This 1965 picture shows something of the bustle of the Admiralty Pier in those days with dock cranes in constant motion and shunters moving goods up and down the quay.

A very early picture dating from 1961 and illustrating the *Koningin Elizabeth* of 1957. Second Class passengers were given far more cover in the post-war Ostend vessels when compared to the *Prince Baudouin* and her sisters.

The third of the class was the *Reine Astrid* of 1958, the first to be built with stabilisers. Remaining in service until 1981, her subsequent career ended in quite a different fashion to that of her sisters.

By 1966, the carriage of freight across the Channel was dramatically increasing. It therefore came as a surprise when Belgian Marine introduced the splendid *Prinses Paola*, the very last traditional passenger only cross-Channel ferry to be built and the final one to remain in service.

The 1970s

Until 1970, SNCF car ferries had operated to Calais while British Rail vessels ran to Boulogne. In that year BR ships supplemented the twin French ferries and increased services there year by year until Boulogne eventually became a secondary route.

The year 1972 saw the end of the fabled Dover-Calais 'Golden Arrow' service and the introduction of a vehicle ferry linkspan at Folkestone. The new ships *Hengist* and *Horsa* displayed 'Sealink' along their sides reflecting the trading partnership between the British, French, Belgian and Dutch fleets. By the end of September, when the 'Arrow' finished, it was no longer possible to travel year-round by passenger steamer to Calais and all services became one class. Two years later a linkspan was opened at the Admiralty Pier at Dover allowing the new generation of Belgian vehicle ferries to carry both cars and freight whilst also connecting with continental boat trains. By the end of the decade there were only two Belgian passenger vessels in operation.

In 1976, the new port of Dunkirk West opened and the Dover train ferries were able to operate a more intensive service while the same year also saw the formation of

Normandy Ferries, a P&O subsidiary operating on the Boulogne link with the Glasgow-registered *Lion*.

She was followed by the Danish-built sisters, *nf Tiger* and *nf Panther* and the Dover-Boulogne route (which had been seen as unprofitable by British Rail) briefly flourished. Throughout the 70s Boulogne once again became an attractive destination but with both Sealink partners and Townsend Thoresen planning new generation ferries, P&O's inability to match them saw a gradual decline throughout the following decade.

The growth of freight on the Zeebrugge link was reflected by the introduction of three new 76 freight unit roll on - roll off ferries between 1975-78 and the eventual stretching of the *Free Enterprise VI* and *Free Enterprise VII*.

Always cash strapped, the joint Sealink fleets converted three stern-loading vessels to drive-through operations but this proved to be very much a stop-gap measure before new tonnage was planned for the early 1980s.

In April 1975, it's refit time again in the Wellington Dock where the *Vortigern* (left - and unusually stern in) dwarfs the train ferry *Anderida*. Acquired new as a replacement for the *Shepperton Ferry* in 1972, the freighter had two sets of railway lines laid on her vehicle deck.

The *St. Patrick* finished service in September 1971 after which she was sold to Greek owners. Here she is berthing at Folkestone during her final month while preliminary work is carried out at the landward berth in preparation for the new car ferry linkspan.

Two days after bowing out on the 'Golden Arrow' service at Dover in August 1972, the *Invicta* is seen arriving at Newhaven for lay-up and sale. The 'Arrow' continued in the hands of the *Maid of Orleans* until the end of September when the fabled service was finally closed.

A memorable day at Folkestone in July 1972 as the new *Hengist* approaches the linkspan from Boulogne on the opening day of the new vehicle services which also ran to Calais and overnight to Ostend. Sadly, in the case of Folkestone, it proved to be too little, too late.

The *Hengist* was joined by her sister ship *Horsa* which, by the time this picture was taken in August 1974, had received much larger name lettering on her bow and stern. The sisters were the first in the railway-owned fleet to carry the word 'Sealink' along their hulls.

The *Horsa's* entry into service in 1972 coincided with the withdrawal of the *Invicta*. Here is the new ship in berth 4 on Dover's Admiralty Pier while the three remaining former Pullman First Class cars are shunted on the quay. The *Reine Astrid* is in berth 3.

The last day of the *Invicta* (8th August 1972) is witnessed by the *Shepperton Ferry* (herself weeks from withdrawal) at berth 5 and the *Maid of Orleans* at number 4. The latter blows off as she is passed by the *Invicta* about to head out into a Channel gale.

Farewell *Shepperton Ferry*! The elderly steamer is seen having recently departed from the Train Ferry Dock at Dover on a routine lunchtime departure for Dunkirk in July 1972. She was finally withdrawn from service in August.

With the *Dover*'s extra car capacity seeing her switched to the Irish Sea, her half sister *Holyhead Ferry I* was moved to the Dover - Boulogne link. This July 1973 picture also shows the recently built Belgian vehicle ferry *Prins Philippe* which had introduced a new funnel design featuring the letters RMT.

The *Maid of Orleans* heading away from the Admiralty Pier in September 1975, shortly before her withdrawal from service and subsequent sale to Spanish breakers.

The train ferry *Anderida* approaching Dover from Dunkirk in July 1976. Purchased off the stocks from Stena Line in 1972, during the late 70s she also saw freight service on Sealink's four Irish Sea services, particularly on the Fishguard - Rosslare route.

The *Normannia* is seen at Boulogne's berth 13 in July 1972. The berth was inaugurated by the *Lord Warden* when new in June 1952 - on the left is the Gare Maritime from which trains crossed Europe to a variety of destinations.

In order to increase lorry capacity on the Dover - Calais service, the *Holyhead Ferry I* was sent to the Tyne in late 1975 to be converted to drive-through operations. Returning in September 1976 and renamed *Earl Leofric*, the steamer (complete with 12 lifeboats) is seen leaving Calais during June 1978.

The *Dover* was sent to Aalborg in Denmark a year later and returned to the Dover - Calais service in July 1977 as the *Earl Siward*. She is seen resting in the Wellington Dock during May 1979.

Replacing the *Maid of Orleans* as the summer only train-connected steamer, came the former Channel Islands steamer *Caesarea*. She operated from both Dover and Folkestone to both Calais and Boulogne and is seen leaving for Boulogne during September 1979.

With the slow Sealink downgrading of their Dover - Boulogne link, in April 1976 the vacuum was filled by the P&O subsidiary Normandy Ferries and their car ferry *Lion* (1967) which, due to political 'troubles', had been withdrawn from the Ardrossan - Belfast service.

The SNCF car ferry *Compiegne* at Dover's berth 4 in August 1976. Notice the rise in deck level under the second and third lifeboats - this following the raising of her after car deck in late 1969 to make her more suitabale for the carriage of freight.

The *Chantilly* is seen off Calais in May 1979. As has been seen elsewhere, both SNCF and the Belgian RMT fleets joined the Sealink consortium and adopted the familar branding. She was also converted to drive-through operations during the winter of 1975-76.

The French answer to the *Vortigern* was the *Chartres* of 1974. Her hull was built to fit the Train Ferry Dock at Dover and she could operate both as a train ferry and a traditional vehicle/ passenger ferry thereby giving her a great deal of versatility. She is seen arriving at Folkestone in August 1974.

Farewell to 'Le Twick'! The ALA train ferry steams out of Dover during her final months in service in 1974 before her sale for scrap in Spain where her sisters had also been broken up. Her period of service had been extended due to the lateness of her replacement.

Here at last - the new *Saint Eloi* about to swing off the Train Ferry Dock on her arrival from Dunkirk in April 1975. She continued in service until 1988 after which she became the seasonal train-connected ferry linking Dover with Calais. In 1989 she was renamed *Channel Entente* before sale to the Isle of Man the following year.

A visit to Ostend during September 1975 saw the sale-listed car ferry *Prinses Josephine Charlotte* (1949) and the passenger vessel *Koning Albert* (1947) tucked away in the inner dock. Two other car ferries were being used on a once a day basis while spare passenger ships were activated as required.

In the hope of winning back some of the freight traffic being lost to Townsend at Zeebrugge, during 1975, RMT introduced the sister ships *Prinses Maria-Esmeralda* and *Princesse Marie-Christine* (pictured) during May and December. A near sister *Prins Albert* joined them in March 1978.

The *Prince Laurent* of 1974 opened the new linkspan on Dover's Admiralty Pier in June so that ferries could load both vehicles and train-connected passengers from the adjacent Marine Station. The 'Laurent' was a sister ship to the *Prins Philippe* but was far more successful having hoistable mezzanine decks.

The *Koningin Fabiola* and (far left) *Artevelde* at Ostend in September 1975. The 'Fabiola' was moving forward to her linkspan to operate a single late afternoon round sailing to Dover. The retention of such a large and inappropriate fleet was to ultimately lead to the downfall of RMT.

Easter 1977 was one of the last outings for the *Koningin Elizabeth* which is seen pulling away from the Admiralty Pier on a lightly loaded mid-morning sailing to Ostend. She was sold with her earlier sister in 1978 when they became Red Sea pilgrim carriers.

The *Autocarrier* towards the end of her career as a Townsend freight ship in July 1973, on the berth at Camber 'A'. As can be seen, her lorry deck was very exposed and was frequently drenched with spray. In later years her after two lifeboats were removed.

Three freight ships, the latter two of which were destined for Dover - Zeebrugge were acquired off the stocks from the SUAG yard at Bremerhaven in 1975/76. The *European Trader* and *European Clearway* (pictured) soon established themselves and the modified *European Enterprise* followed during 1978.

Seen from the *Chartres* during May 1979, the *Free Enterprise II* swings off her berth on a misty afternoon. This was the final summer that the first three 'Free Enterprise' ships operated together. She was eventually disposed of in the following year and later saw service in Italy.

The addition of a lounge between her funnel and bridge did little to improve the looks of the *Free Enterprise III*. The ship is seen arriving at Calais in May 1979. She was sold to Malta in 1984 before a disastrous association with the Isle of Man Steam Packet Company and a further sale to Saudi Arabia.

The *Free Enterprise V* entered service in May 1970 and is seen at Dover's berth 3 in June 1978. The bow door is open in order to help disperse vehicle fumes after the ship had unloaded on her arrival from Zeebrugge.

In July 1973 the *Dover* (later *Earl Siward*) heads out of Dover for Calais as the *Free Enterprise VI* swings in the lee of the Southern Breakwater before coming astern to discharge from Zeebrugge. After having been returned to the builders, the 'FE VI' had entered service in June 1972.

The *Free Enterprise VII* at berth 4 in August 1976 having entered service in February 1973. Freight traffic on the Zeebrugge link grew to such an extent that plans were drawn up to stretch both the 'FE VI' and 'FE VII' to double their lorry deck capacity.

The 1980s

The start of the decade saw a period of intense competition on the Dover – Calais service with both Townsend Thoresen and Sealink introducing a trio of large double-decked drive-through ferries.

Steam bowed out with the final departure of the *Caledonian Princess* in 1981 and in 1984 the company was denationalised and sold to Sea Containers of Bermuda. Trading as Sealink British Ferries, the brash American style of management soon upset the Belgian partners who objected to SeaCo's stated intention to take 50% of the traffic on the Ostend route. An unholy row developed during which time Sealink British Ferries' ships were barred from entering Ostend or Zeebrugge. In an attempt to win back lost freight traffic, SeaCo introduced two totally unsuitable deep-sea freight vessels and placed them on the Dunkirk West link.

The Belgians then did the unthinkable and entered into a new trading agreement with Townsend Thoresen in 1987 after which time their fleet adopted TT orange hulls. The final passenger-only ship, the *Prinses Paola*, was withdrawn

from service at the end of the 1987 season.

On the Boulogne route, Townsend Thoresen had taken over P&O Normandy Ferries and their three ships in 1985.

With the Channel Tunnel under construction, in 1987 Townsend Thoresen introduced a new generation of 'Chunnel Beaters' in the *Pride of Dover* and *Pride of Calais*. Towards the end of the previous year, the company had been taken over by the P&O Group and within months were faced with the disaster at Zeebrugge. P&O distanced themselves from the previous operators by launching P&O European Ferries and a new dark blue livery, renaming the ships 'Pride of' and dropping the 'Free Enterprise' titles.

Sealink British Ferries' response to the 'Chunnel Beaters' was the purchase of two deep-sea ro-ro ships which they sent to Bremerhaven for rebuilding. They emerged as the *Fantasia* and *Fiesta*.

At rest in the Wellington Dock during March 1980, the passenger steamer *Caesarea* prepares for her final season in operation. To mark her passing, a special series of 'Farewell crossings' were organised culminating in an RNLI Charter from Folkestone to Boulogne during early October.

The much-travelled turbine steamer *Caledonian Princess* spent her final 1981 season in service operating the *Caesarea*'s old rosters on the train-connected services. Although recalled to the Channel Islands, during which time the *Free Enterprise III* was chartered, she survived until September, eventually becoming a night club on the Tyne.

The closure of the Harwich-Zeebrugge train ferry service in January 1987 made redundant the 1963 train ferry *Cambridge Ferry* which commenced service at Dover in March. The vessel later moved to the Irish Sea in a freight role.

The *Earl Leofric* (left) and *Earl Siward* laid up for sale in the River Ouse at Newhaven during 1981. The former was scrapped while the latter was sold to Greek owners before becoming a floating night club in the north-east.

The *Hengist* alongside at Calais in June 1982 before the service from Folkestone was axed in June 1984. Ostend sailings closed the following March after which both she and the *Horsa* concentrated on the Boulogne link which became their home from home until their untimely withdrawal in 1991.

In 1984 Sealink UK Ltd was privatised and acquired by Sea Containers of Bermuda. A new livery had been adopted in readiness for privatisation after which the company traded as Sealink British Ferries. Here the *Hengist* hurries out of Boulogne in April 1986.

The Great Storm of October 1987 has gone down in the annals of British weather forecasting. With Folkestone Harbour station and the *St. Christopher* both badly damaged and the *Hengist* aground, the *Horsa* was switched to operate between Dover and Calais. The freighter *Seafreight Highway* lies on the Eastern Arm after demolishing the cafe on the end of the Prince of Wales' Pier.

Winter reliefs at Folkestone provided the port with spare tonnage from elsewhere in the Sealink fleet. During October 1982, the Weymouth - Cherbourg summer ferry *Ailsa Princess* made her first visit to the port but was unable to use her bow visor.

Laid up in the Wellington Dock during February 1981, the *Anderida* was later joined by near sister *Ulidia* before both were sold in October. Leaving Dover as the *Truck Trader*, the *Anderida* was appropriately renamed *Sealink* for her eventual service in New Zealand.

On charter to Sealink for their Dover - Boulogne route in August 1982 is the Belgian car ferry *Roi Baudouin* which is seen entering the Camber. Later in the year she served the Folkestsone - Boulogne link and redundant in the Ostend fleet, the ship was sold to Greek owners in the following year.

The arrival of the Belfast-built *St. Anselm* and *St.Christopher* in 1980/81 was the final throw of the nationalised railway company to compete with their rivals Townsend Thoresen. They proved to be fine ships to handle although their accommodation was disappointing. The *St. Anselm* leaves Dover for Calais in June 1982.

In 1983 the pair were sent back to their builders for extensions to their passenger accommodation which greatly improved matters on board and increased capacity to 1,400. Later plans to stretch the twins were shelved. The *St. Christopher* leaves Calais in November 1985.

The fourth of the Harland & Wolff quartet, the *St. David*, was sent down to Dover from Holyhead to cover for the refit of the *St. Christopher* and is seen at Calais on the occasion of her first visit in March 1983. She was the final cross-Channel vessel built for Sealink and survived as the *Stena Caledonia* until 2011.

During the 80s, the *Vortigern* was the third ship to the *Hengist* and *Horsa* on the Folkestone - Boulogne route although train ferry duties were occasionally required for the Dunkirk link. Her former side-loading garage (entrance above the 'k' of 'Sealink') was converted into a lounge during 1978.

Farewell *Vortigern*! The ship is seen arriving at Boulogne on her final advertsied sailing in September 1986 although was required for refit periods. She was even chartered for Townsend Thoresen's Dover - Boulogne service after the loss of their *Herald of Free Enterprise*.

The freighter *European Trader* at anchor in Dover Harbour during summer 1986 as SNCF's *Cote d'Azur* arrives from Calais. The ship had entered service in late 1981 as the French contribution to Sealink's 'Flagship Service'.

The Dover - Zeebrugge freighter *European Enterprise* (renamed *European Endeavour* in 1987) was built to Townsend Thoresen's modified design after the introduction of the 'Trader' and the 'Clearway'. Eventually replaced by larger tonnage, all three ships finished service in the North Channel operating from Larne to Cairnryan.

A powerful view of the *Free Enterprise VI* leaving Dover for Zeebrugge in October 1984, the year before she was sent to Bremerhaven for stretching.

The *Free Enterprise VII* had her main mast sited further aft than her earlier sisters and was therefore easy to identify. She shares this picture with the Dover Harbour Board's tug *Diligent* (1958) which with her sister *Dominant* assisted in keeping the ferry fleets running during inclement weather.

In 1985, one third of the Camber was infilled to provide greater standage space for freight. The *European Enterprise* lays by on the new quay as the *Free Enterprise IV* arrives bow first from Boulogne at the original berth 2. The Camber was eventually completely infilled during 1988.

In June 1985 the *Free Enterprise V* was back at Dover from Portsmouth during the time when both the Zeebrugge vessels *Free Enterprise VI* and *Free Enterprise VII* were undergoing stretching at Bremerhaven.

The *Free Enterprise VII* heading for Dover from Zeebrugge in May 1987. Following the loss of the 'Herald' earlier in March, little time was lost in applying the P&O pale blue funnel and flag. The stretching of both ships increased lorry capacity from 24 to 60.

The last of the 'Free Enterprise' series was the 'FE VIII' which was 12 metres longer than the rest of her class. Believing that she was too long to berth safely at Calais, the ship was used exclusively on the Zeebrugge link. Notice the dent in her bow-visor which was always vulnerable.

Another incomer required to assist during the stretching of the 'FE VI' and 'FE VII' was the former Atlantic Steam Navigation Co's *Gaelic Ferry* which is seen alongside the new quay in the Camber during September 1985.

The *Spirit of Free Enterprise* was the lead ship for a trio of, what turned out to be, quite controversial ferries which were built in Bremerhaven and entered service during 1980. Here she is leaving Calais during her first week in service in January 1980 - outside deck space was sadly minimal.

The *Herald of Free Enterprise* was the second ship of the trio which introduced neat-stow bow doors which slid around the ships' bows in place of the usual up and over bow visors. It was the failure to close these doors which lead to the 'Herald's' loss off Zeebrugge on 6th March 1987 - the port's worst ever ferry disaster.

Not everyone was happy to see the name Townsend Thoresen disappear as witnessed by the less than successful attempt to cover the company name on the hull of the *Pride of Free Enterprise* - the third of the 'Spirit' trio which is alongside at Calais in October 1987.

The aftermath of the 'Herald' disaster was a difficult time for P&O who had taken over Townsend Thoresen's parent company (the European Ferries Group) in the previous December. The entry into service of the first of the 'Chunnel Beaters', the *Pride of Dover* in June 1987 was understandably a very low key affair. Here is the ship leaving Calais in October, still with her orange hull.

The *Pride of Calais* entered service in December 1987 and is seen at Calais berth 6 on the occasion of her maiden voyage. She replaced the *Free Enterprise IV* in service.

The ALA train ferry *Saint Eloi* is seen nearing Dunkirk in May 1986. Dover's original Train Ferry Dock finally closed in May 1988 after which she was initially chartered to SNCF for the seasonal Calais - Dover train-connected services.

SNCF's *Cote d'Azur* is seen off Dover in June 1987 with the new application of the 'Sealink' trading name following the Sea Containers' takeover of Sealink UK Ltd three years earlier.

The *Champs Elysees* joined the Sealink fleet in October 1984, replacing the *Chantilly* in the local fleet. An unsuccessful and brief attempt was made to revive the Dover - Boulogne route and in summer 1990 she was switched to the Dieppe - Newhaven route.

The elderly train ferry *Saint-Germain* was built in Denmark and entered service from Dunkirk to Dover in 1951. She served faithfully until her withdrawal in 1987, occasionally being used in the 50s and 60s as a car ferry on the Dover - Boulogne/Calais links.

The *Transcontainer I* was originally built in 1969 as a freighter operating between Dunkirk and Harwich but in 1974 her main vehicle deck was fitted with railway lines. Late in her career she was transferred to the Dover link and is seen during 1986, her last season in service.

Latterly used on the secondary Dover - Boulogne route and for reliefs at Calais, the *Compiegne* was by June 1980 (when this image was taken) somewhat out of her league. After a number of false finishes, she was finally withdrawn and sold to Greek owners late in 1981.

The *Chartres* had been transferred to the Dieppe - Newhaven route in 1982 but was brought back to cover train ferry reliefs in November 1986 when this picture was taken. She eventually returned to Calais for the 1990 season.

The train ferry *Nord Pas-de-Calais* was due to enter service in 1987. However, the Great Storm of October that year caused so much damage to her new linkspan and associated workings on the Admiralty Pier at Dover that she was initially used as a freighter on the Calais link. She is seen at Calais in May 1988, the same month that she commenced her Dunkirk sailings.

The RMT passenger ferry *Prinses Paola* is seen approaching Ostend in September 1986. Sealink British Ferries had previously expressed a wish to take over 50% of the trade on the Ostend link as a result of which RMT joined forces with Townsend Thoresen in 1986. The beautiful 'Paola' was withdrawn in September the following year.

Farewell *Reine Astrid*! The ship is seen leaving Dover on one of her final sailings at the end of September 1981 - a day of gales and delays. Rather than sell her, RMT ordered major surgery and in May 1983 the 'ship' reappeared as Dover's floating pontoon for the new jetfoil service.

Could this ever have been the *Reine Astrid*? The jetfoil *Princesse Clementine* is seen leaving Dover in September 1985. The Boeing craft crossed in 100 minutes and an excellent service was provided. They were unfortunately very expensive to operate and only a nationalised ferry company could afford to employ them.

Looking a little shabby, the RMT car ferry *Prins Philippe* arrives at Dover in April 1983. As the first of a new generation of RMT car ferries, much was expected of her but her fixed mezzanine deck proved to be her Achilles' heel and she was disposed of after just 13 years.

The *Prins Albert* was a slightly modified version of the *Prinses Maria-Esmeralda* of 1975 but was fitted with an extra lounge (aft, lower) at the expense of garage space. She too was stretched in 1986 thereby increasing her freight capacity from 46 to 55 units.

The *Reine Astrid* (2) was chartered from Stena Line in 1982 to provide RMT with much needed freight capacity on their Ostend link. With capacity for as many as 43 units, she was purchased in the following year, although her slow speed frequently produced 5 hour crossings.

The *Prince Laurent* at lay by in Ostend during November 1985 after having just been repainted in Townsend Thoresen orange livery. Towards the end of her career she frequently operated as a passenger vessel before her sale to Greece during 1991.

P&O's Glasgow registered *Lion* leaving the Camber at Dover for Boulogne in May 1980. Painted in the pale blue ferry livery two years previously, great attempts were made to improve on-board standards but the ship was always too small for major modifications.

The *nf Panther* (1972) joined the P&O fleet in 1980. Like her sister, the *nf Tiger*, she was originally built for internal service in Denmark being named *Djursland*. After her sale in 1987, she continued in P&O service operating as the *St. Sunniva* to the Orkneys and Shetlands.

The *nf Tiger* is seen approaching Boulogne in April 1986 following the Townsend Thoresen takeover of the English Channel ferry business in January 1985. Townsend lost little time in replacing the former P&O ships with the *Free Enterprise IV* and *Free Enterprise V*.

The 1990s

Most developments centred around the threat posed by the opening of the Channel Tunnel 'shuttle' service in 1994. Company developments continued apace with the acquisition of Sealink British Ferries by the Swedish ferry giant Stena Line in 1990. Having paid more than the company was worth, Stena immediately looked for savings and closed the Folkestone – Boulogne link at the end of the following year. Sealink was now known as Sealink Stena although this was modified to Stena Sealink in 1992 and simply Stena four years later. The year 1996 also saw the French split with Stena Line and the formation of SeaFrance on the Calais link.

September 1993 had seen the ending of the Dover Western Docks – Calais Maritime train-connected services and the withdrawal of the *Chartres*.

The unhappy trading agreement between the Belgian Government fleet (RMT) and P&O Ferries ended in 1994 when the Ostend service was switched to Ramsgate from where it lingered for another three years before its inevitable closure. The ending of the Belgian Ostend service saw the RMT fleet laid up in Dunkirk East. P&O promptly chartered the former fleet flagship *Prins Filip* before introducing her as the *Pride of Aquitaine* on the Calais service in 1998.

Another route to close was that between Dover and Boulogne which P&O axed in 1993 to strengthen their position on the Calais link where they were running their own seamless shuttle in preparation for the Tunnel's opening.

In a bid to fight the Channel Tunnel, in 1998 P&O Ferries and Stena Line entered into a joint venture with P&O taking a 60% share. Ships were painted in P&O blue with both house flags on their funnels while ship names were prefixed 'P&OSL' to denote the joint nature of the service.

On her return from the Dieppe - Newhaven service, the *Chartres* was chartered by the British-owned French subsidiary ALA to operate the seasonal Dover - Calais rail-connected services. She is seen arriving at the Admiralty Pier in August 1993 one month before the service was axed and the ship was sold.

The purchase of two Bulgarian deep-sea roll on - roll off ferries in 1988, was to be Sealink British Ferries' response to Townsend Thoresen's purpose-built 'Chunnel Beaters'. After a major conversion at Bremerhaven, the *Fantasia* entered service on the Dover - Calais route in March 1990.

In June 1990, the much travelled former Thoresen ferry *Viking II* was briefly switched to the Dover Strait to provide cover on the Folkestone - Boulogne route. As the *Earl William* she had maintained the Channel Islands routes although the 26-year-old ferry was sale lsited by this time.

The *St. Christopher* is seen arriving at Calais in November 1990 during her final period in local service. With the Stena takeover of Sealink British Ferries, she was renamed *Stena Antrim* and switched to the North Channel route between Stranraer and Belfast.

Sister ship *St. Anselm* was renamed *Stena Cambria* and eventually moved to the Holyhead station although she made numerous reappearances back at Dover. In this wide-angled view, she powers into Calais on an afternoon sailing from Dover.

Stena Line paid £259 million for Sealink British Ferries and the cost-saving exercise Operation Benchmark was inevitably imposed. The Folkestone - Boulogne service became a victim of this rationalisation and the *Stena Horsa* closed the route on the last day of 1991.

Stena Line introduced the deep-sea ro-pax vessel *Stena Challenger* onto the Dover - Calais route in June 1981 but after six months moved her to the Dunkirk West link. The 100 lorry ship was switched to the Irish Sea in 1996 before her sale to Canadian interests four years later.

At the same time as the 'Challenger's' introduction, the *Stena Invicta* (1985) was brought in to boost passenger traffic on the Dover - Calais link. As the former Danish ferry *Peder Paas*, she managed this well but with only one deck of freight (36 lorries), she was a far from successful addition to the fleet.

In 1992, Stena Line rebranded their new company 'Stena Sealink Line' before a complete change to 'Stena Line' in January 1996. Thus the final vestiges of the nationalised railway era came to an end as the Swedish company boasted, "We know how to run ferries".

The *Stena Fantasia* as she appeared in October 1997. Both she and her French sister ship *Fiesta/SeaFrance Cezanne* could never hide the fact that they were conversions but their interior design was innovative, setting new trends in cross-Channel comfort and experience.

The *Stena Empereur* (1983) was the former *Stena Jutlandica* which had been built at Dunkirk for the Gothenburg - Frederikshavn link. Arriving at Dover in August 1996, she was not ideally suited to the intensive operations experienced on the Dover Strait but nevertheless always looked impressive.

Vehicle carrying cross-Channel hovercraft commenced service in 1968 but the formation of Hoverspeed in 1981 saw a brief window in which their operation threatened the traditional ferry industry. Lack of development, escalating fuel costs and small payloads eventually saw them off. Here *The Prince of Wales* (1977) enters Dover in March 1991.

In 1991 Hoverspeed introduced the first of their 80 car, 74 metre catamarans on the services from Folkestone and Dover to Calais and Boulogne. The *Hoverspeed France* is seen alongside at Boulogne in September 1992.

The *SeaCat Calais* (ex *SeaCat Tasmania*) moving alongside the Prince of Wales' Pier at Dover in August 1993. The constant changes of livery, names and routes did little to improve the popularity of these craft although as drive-through vessels, they were at least most suited to the busy Dover - Calais route.

In May 1990, the *Cote d'Azur* is seen approaching Calais from Dover in the new livery of her operating company SPN. At a time when Stena Line had removed their former British operating partners from the Dover Strait, the French retained their vessels from the same era long afterwards.

Taken three months prior to the previous shot, the *Champs Elysees* is still seen in the earlier company livery. This was to be her last season of her first spell on the Calais - Dover route as with the arrival of the *Fiesta* later that year, she was transferred to Dieppe.

The train ferry *Nord Pas-de-Calais* in the SPN livery arriving at Dover's Admiralty Pier in March 1994. Freight was carried on her upper deck whilst the railway wagons filled the deck below. Inevitably, the opening of the Channel Tunnel affected loadings but she soldiered on until the link's closure in December 1995.

The inevitable split between Stena Line and their French Dover - Calais partners occurred in January 1996. At this time the French formed SeaFrance and reclaimed two of their vessels from Dieppe which had latterly been on charter to Stena. The *SeaFrance Monet* (ex *Stena Londoner/Versailles*) swings at Calais in March 1999.

The former *Champs Elysees/Stena Parisien* became the *SeaFrance Manet* on her return from the Dieppe - Newhaven route in January 1997.

The *Fiesta* was renamed *SeaFrance Cezanne* at the same time and was by far the largest of the SeaFrance fleet. The huge amount of outside deck space between the funnels made her a popular choice for cross-Channel excursions.

The Ostend - Dover link was greatly boosted by the introduction of their *Prins Filip* in May 1992. She was a splendid ship and displayed the best that the Belgian tax payer could afford. She is seen under the course of construction at her builder's yard at Temse during March 1991.

With the formation of P&O European ferries in October 1987, Belgian partners RMT adapted their own livery to something corresponding that of P&O. The *Princesse Marie-Christine* enters Ostend in July 1990. Her former Thoresen orange paint is evident along her waterline.

The *Reine Astrid* (2) about to berth at Ostend in February 1991 showing the attractive livery of the re-branded Ostend - Dover Line. The fleet used side doors to discharge cars from their upper vehicle decks while freight rolled off across the traditional linkspan.

The *European Clearway* seen at berth 1 on the Eastern Arm during March 1991 towards the end of her time on the Dover Strait. Both she and her sisters had greatly contributed to the success of the Zeebrugge link and much larger replacements were then being built at Bremerhaven.

The *European Pathway* (1991) was the second of a projected quartet of ro-ro ships for the Zeebrugge link. In the event the fourth became the *Pride of Burgundy* and this ship too was later converted for passenger use on the Calais link. The 'Pathway' arrives at Zeebrugge in August 1992.

Portsmouth's *Pride of Winchester* (1976) deputised on the Dover - Calais link during late 1989 and is pictured alongside berth 2 in the French port. Built for the Felixstowe - Zeebrugge link as the *Viking Viscount*, the ship was transferred to the south coast in 1986.

The *Pride of Burgundy* leaving Calais in March 1994. Intended to be the *European Causeway* and used as a freight ship on the Zeebrugge link, she was modified on the stocks to provide passenger capacity for the Calais service. This hastily considered conversion has not proved to be particularly successful.

The *Pride of Dover* approaching Calais in the livery of P&O European Ferries during May 1990. Being purpose-built for this most demanding of routes, both she and her sister proved to be outstanding successes although with low interior deck heads, their passenger accommodation was initially rather gloomy.

The former *Spirit of Free Enterprise* was renamed *Pride of Kent* at the formation of P&O European Ferries in October 1987. This July 1991 picture shows her prior to being sent to Palermo in Sicily during 1991-92 in order to have a new 30 metre section added thereby making her more compatible with the new 'Chunnel Beaters'.

Here is the *Pride of Kent* in November 1997 looking extremely ungainly as she leaves Dover for Calais. The stretching was not deemed a success and the third of the class - now named *Pride of Bruges* - was not converted.

The *Pride of Canterbury* was the *Free Enterprise VIII* and is seen leaving Boulogne for Dover in September 1992. P&O closed the link without warning in January 1993 after which the ship was sold to Greek owners.

In order to combat the threat of the Channel Tunnel, a 'joint venture' between P&O and Stena Line commenced in March 1998. The *Pride of Bruges* (ex *Pride of Free Enterprise*) displays the joint livery as she sweeps into Calais in July 1998. In December she was renamed *P&OSL Picardy*.

The *Stena Empereur* was renamed *P&OSL Provence* and is seen storming out of Calais in August 1999. The addition of her 'cow-catcher' in order to effect a good port fit in Calais always created a good bow wave.

The 2000s

The first year of the new millennium saw the withdrawal of the twin hovercraft on the Dover – Calais service. Theirs was a niche market and although other high-speed craft continued, the Hoverspeed services ended in 2005.

The joint-venture between P&O Ferries and Stena Line ended in 2002 with the two remaining former Stena Line units in the fleet being replaced in the following year by converted freight ships from the Zeebrugge service which had closed in December 2002.

The Danish company Maersk re-opened the Dunkirk West route in March 2000 with the Spanish-built *Northern Merchant* which was later joined by two more sister ships from the class of four. The success of the service saw three purpose-built ships enter service in 2005/06 before both they and the route were acquired by DFDS Seaways in 2010.

Boulogne welcomed a year round fast ferry service in 2004. This was operated by SpeedFerries with their *SpeedOne* and for a while the venture flourished before succumbing four years later. Then in 2009 the French LD Lines appeared in the Dover Strait with the spare Newhaven – Dieppe vessel

Cote d'Albatre which also opened up an overnight sailing to Dieppe. Later that year the fast craft *Norman Arrow* joined the link but was removed after five months. The *Norman Spirit* (ex *Prins Filip/Pride of Aquitaine*) then appeared followed by two of the *Northern Merchant* class of ro-pax ferries. Boulogne opened a new port in the outer harbour during 2009 but the chaotic venture and optimism soon foundered and the service closed in September 2010.

The French state-owned subsidiary SeaFrance continued to make huge losses and was sale listed during 2010. The fleet was reduced to a minimum and the inevitable redundancies caused unprecedented and unresolved problems between management and the trade unions.

P&O Ferries introduced the largest cross-Channel ferries yet during 2011 when the Finnish-built *Spirit of Britain* and *Spirit of France* (47,592 gross tons) entered service. These impressive ferries (capable of carrying 3.5 km of traffic) dwarfed their predecessors and being built to 'Dover-Max' specification, will set the trend for the foreseeable future.

Although Stena Line closed the traditional Folkestone - Boulogne service in 1991, Hoverspeed reopened it with a catamaran in the following April. This service eventually succumbed in October 2000 and the last ship to sail on the route was the freighter *Neptunia* which is seen in September 2000. The link closed in June 2001.

Farewell Hovercraft! *The Princess Anne* is seen leaving Dover on one of her final flights to Calais on 1st October 2000. With her sister *The Princess Margaret*, theirs was a niche market and although the service continued with a variety of fast craft, continued losses saw its closure in November 2005.

The *Diamant* (pictured) and her sister *Rapide* took over the operation of the Ramsgate - Ostend service after the closure of the RMT link in February 1997. Continuing to make losses, the Holyman vessels were acquired by Hoverspeed who briefly re-introduced the historic link to Dover in March 1998 before it too closed three years later.

The *SeaCat Danmark* leaving Calais in May 2003. The 74 metre craft was introduced in 1992 having been christened *Hoverspeed Belgium* and entering service as the *Hoverspeed Boulogne*. She reopened the Folkestone - Boulogne service in April 1991. Between 1993-96 she operated on the Kattegat, hence the adoption of this name.

In May 2004 the Danish company SpeedFerries began operating their 86 metre craft *SpeedOne* (1997) on the Dover - Boulogne route and for a while, they caused quite a stir. Aggressive marketing and attractive fare structures saw the company briefly prosper before the inevitable occurred in November 2008.

In February 2009, LD Lines introduced the spare Dieppe ferry *Cote d'Albatre* onto the Boulogne - Dover route where she is seen arriving at berth 1 on her maiden commercial crossing. Meanwhile the *SeaFrance Cezanne* (operating in a freight mode) enters the port on her penultimate day in service.

The introduction of the 112 metre catamaran *Norman Arrow* in June 2009 looked to guarantee LD Lines a bright future on the Boulogne service. The craft is seen arriving at Dover from her Tasmanian builders but after just five months, she was withdrawn from service, LD claiming that she was unable to carry sufficient freight.

LD Lines' next move was to transfer the *Norman Spirit* from their Portsmouth - Le Havre route to Dover - Boulogne in November 2009. The ship was the former RMT *Prins Filip* and latterly P&O's chartered *Pride of Aquitaine* but in her LD role she lasted just four months. The *Pride of Calais* is seen loading at berth 3.

In March 2010 LD Lines introduced a further new ship, the *Norman Trader* (ex *Brave Merchant* - 1999) which is seen at berth 1 in June 2010. She was later joined by her sister ship *Norman Bridge* (ex *Dawn Merchant*). The service closed completely in September 2010.

In May 2010, the *Ostend Spirit* (ex *Prins Filip* etc) was switched from her unsuccessful Ramsgate to Ostend joint service to cover the *Norman Bridge* at Dover. The whole episode had become something of a farce.

The route between Dover and Dunkirk West was resurrected by the Danish company Maersk in March 2000 when under their Norfolkline subsidiary they chartered the new Merchant Ferries ro-pax *Northern Merchant*. Joined by sistership *Midnight Merchant* (pictured) in October, the service proved to be an immediate success. The ship later returned to Dover as P&O's second named *European Endeavour*.

A third sister ship, the *Dawn Merchant* joined the Norfolkline fleet in September 2002 although unlike her sisters she was never fitted with a 'cow-catcher' for drive-through operations. She appeared later at Dover as the *Norman Bridge*.

The success of the new Dunkirk West link soon saw orders being made for three identical sisters from South Korea. Entering service in July 2006, the third of the trio was the *Maersk Dover* which is seen entering Dunkirk West in December 2006 in her original livery.

The *Maersk Dover* is seen again at Dover's berth 3 in September 2008 and wearing her owner's modified livery. The light blue hull below the belting always showed the rust and the adoption of red helped to cover this. As for the name brand - it allowed it to be seen above the piers at Dover.

The *Maersk Delft* was the second of the trio in service in February 2006. Although impressive looking vessels, they were lightly built and frequently require the use of tugs when berthing at Dover. Some 120 freight vehicles can be carried.

The lead ship of the trio was the *Maersk Dunkerque* which entered service in November 2005. She is seen at Dover's berth 2 during June 2009. The forward atrium below the bridge is particularly impressive housing the drivers' cafeteria (above) and the passengers' cafeteria (below). Passengers and their vehicles have their own dedicated decks.

DFDS Seaways took over the Maersk ferry operations in June 2010 and here is the former *Maersk Delft* - now *Maersk Seaways* - sporting her new name and intermediate livery before full repainting the following January.

The *Dunkerque Seaways* is seen in her full DFDS Seaways livery in March 2011 although, in common with her sisters, patches of the former pale blue hull paint were already starting to show through.

The *SeaFrance Renoir* received £5 million improvements to her after passenger accommodation during her 1995 refit. With SeaFrance making huge losses towards the end of the decade she continued in service after both the 'Manet' and 'Cezanne' had been withdrawn, finally bowing out in May 2009.

The *SeaFrance Manet* was withdrawn from service in April 2008 and eventually sold to Stena Line for their North Channel link. Here she is laid up in Calais with the funnel of the new *SeaFrance Moliere* appearing from behind her bow-visor.

The smallest ferry in the Dover Strait with the longest name! The *SeaFrance Nord Pas-de-Calais* was used in a freight capacity after the withdrawal of the Dover - Dunkirk West train ferry service in December 1995. She is seen from Calais beach in September 2008.

The *SeaFrance Cezanne* outlived her sister, the former *Fantasia*, in local service by almost six years. Following her withdrawal in February 2009, she began a long lay-up period in Dunkirk before being sold with the 'Renoir' during summer 2011.

The *SeaFrance Rodin* was built in Finland in 2001 and brought much required new tonnage to the SeaFrance fleet. She is seen swinging off her berth at Dover in August 2008. Her passenger accommodation is asymmetrical and the large atrium windows on her starboard side are not duplicated on her port side.

A sister ship, the *SeaFrance Berlioz* joined the SeaFrance fleet in April 2005. With her bridge window glazing bars painted black, she is easily recognisable from the 'Rodin' and her interior is also much brighter. The sisters are two of the best appointed ships in the Eastern Channel and carry 120 lorries.

The former Superfast ship *Superfast X* (2002) was acquired by SeaFrance in 2007 and following her costly conversion to a day ship at Dunkirk the *SeaFrance Moliere* entered service the following October. The ship is far from ideal for the busy Dover - Calais link and cost the company dearly at a time when they were attempting to claw back the huge financial losses that they had accrued.

Farewell *PO Canterbuy* - ex *Fantasia*! Following the demise of the P&O Stena 'joint venture' in October 2002 the ship was briefly renamed *PO Canterbury* before her replacement by the new *Pride of Canterbury* (the former Zeebrugge freight ship *European Pathway*). She is seen in her final weekend of service in May 2003.

The *Pride of Calais* at Calais in September 2008. The ship is expected to be withdrawn from service following the arrival of the new *Spirit of France* in late 2011.

The *Pride of Dover* in her revised livery with the blue hull colour lowered which the fleet received during winter 2002-03. In preparation for the arrival of the new *Spirit of Britain*, the 'Dover' completed her final voyages in December 2010 before being sent for lay-up at Tilbury.

The *Pride of Burgundy* swinging at Dover during September 2009. Lacking the range of on-board facilities of her fleet companions, the ship has recently served in a reduced capacity.

The *Pride of Canterbury* (ex *European Pathway*) was converted from a freight ship at Bremerhaven in 2002-03 and replaced the former Stena ship *PO Canterbury* (ex *Fantasia*) in the fleet.

Sister ship *Pride of Kent* (2) replaced the former *Spirit of Free Enterprise/Pride of Kent* in June 2003 after her own conversion from a freight ship during which time she had operated as the *European Highway*. She is seen leaving Calais in January 2011.

The freighter *European Seaway* was the first of four ships intended for the Zeebrugge service and which were built at Bremerhaven during 1991-92. As such she was the only one not converted to passenger use and after the closure of the Belgian link in December 2002, she worked full time to Calais. She was withdrawn in September 2011 and laid up at Tilbury.

At a time when P&O Ferries required extra freight capacity at Dover and a reserve ship for their Dublin link, the *European Endeavour* (2) was purchased. Arriving at Dover in January 2008, she was the former *Midnight Merchant* that had previously worked the Dunkirk West route for Maersk. She sailed for lay-up in May 2010 and is presently on the Dublin link.

The arrival of the *Spirit of Britain* in January 2011 heralded the start of a new era for P&O Ferries. The largest cross-Channel vessel ever built, at 47,592 gross tons she would dwarf such ferries as the *Normannia* (2,219 gross tons - see page 6). The Port of Dover and its ferries move on.

Due in service in September 2011, the *Spirit of France* was delayed at her Finnish builders due to excessive vibration problems which had also caused problems with her sister during her first season in service. *(STX Europe)*

Index

During November 1986, the *Vortigern* was deputising for a final time on the Calais link. The *European Clearway* is seen at the Camber 'B' freight berth with the *St. Christopher* laid up nearby. Out on the Eastern Arm is the *Free Enterprise VI*.